'He Lost Himself Completely'

## About the Author

Professor Brendan Kelly is associate clinical professor of psychiatry at University College Dublin and consultant psychiatrist at the Mater Misericordiae University Hospital. He holds masters degrees in epidemiology (MSc), healthcare management (MA) and Buddhist studies (MA). In addition to his medical degree (MB BCh BAO), he holds doctorates in medicine (MD), history (PhD), governance (DGov) and law (PhD). He has authored and co-authored over 180 peer-reviewed papers and over 300 non-peer-reviewed papers, as well as various book chapters and books. He is editor-in-chief of the *Irish Journal of Psychological Medicine.*

# 'HE LOST HIMSELF COMPLETELY'

*Shell Shock and Its Treatment at Dublin's Richmond War Hospital, 1916-19*

Brendan Kelly

The Liffey Press

Published by
The Liffey Press Ltd
Raheny Shopping Centre, Second Floor
Raheny, Dublin 5, Ireland
www.theliffeypress.com

A catalogue record of this book is
available from the British Library.

ISBN 978-1-908308-63-4

Printed in Ireland by SprintPrint

# Contents

*Dedication*

This book is dedicated to my parents

# Foreword

I have no idea when you will be reading this foreword. But whatever the day, here is a test for you. Put the word 'shell shock' into Google News. I guarantee that you will get a string of hits.

Today, as I write this piece (1 July 2014), shell shock has once again swept across the sports field (although this may be because we are in the middle of the World Cup and England have again lost a cricket series), but basketball players are also seemingly particularly vulnerable. Also today, house-buyers, particularly in London and the South East, are again experiencing an epidemic of shell shock, as has been the case now for a few years. Perhaps less predictably, the job of a movie reviewer has suddenly become associated with shell shock – quite why seeing *Rich Girl*, *Jersey Boys* or *How to Train your Dragon: II* should lead to this remains a mystery.

All of this would have come as some surprise to, for example, Gunner GH – who was admitted to the Richmond War Hospital in 1918 with depression, worries, pain and 'bursting noises in the head'. In addition, in his dreams 'he imagines he is running'. All of this came after he had been caught in the middle of a field, out in the open, under heavy shell fire.

And likewise Private JK, who was admitted after being 'blown up and buried for 36 hours' in the Ypres salient in 1918.

Just pause for a moment and reflect on what being 'buried for 36 hours' actually means. Little wonder that Private JK, like Gunner GH and many others who were admitted to the Richmond War Hospital, was diagnosed with shell shock.

But if shell shock is now part of modern language and seemingly an inevitable part of political life – Nick Clegg in particular seems to lurch from one episode of shell shock to another, if one believes the journalists, and Ed Miliband likewise – there are two places in which mention of shell shock is noticeable by its absence. These are in contemporary medical textbooks and in military discourse. Even before the end of the First World War, shell shock had fallen out of favour, being, for example, banned as a diagnostic label by the Adjutant General of the British Army in 1917, whilst the War Office enquiry into shell shock, established after the end of the war to report on the past and future management of shell shock, concluded that the term was not just a misnomer but worse, because it carried with it the suggestion that shell shock was a physical disorder like any other wound caused by the exploding shell, it did more harm than good. Shell shock was replaced in both military and medical discourse by a variety of other labels, most of which, such as battle fatigue and the like, attempted to avoid any pathological implications.

Professor Brendan Kelly's invaluable monograph goes easy on too many contemporary references, perhaps because there are just so many of them. But it is striking just how familiar are many of the issues, debates and problems that confronted the Richmond War Hospital between 1916 and 1919. Arguments about treatments, diagnosis, responsibility, secondary gain, ethics and politics all seem familiar and, of course, money. Admitting soldiers was a very good financial deal for the managers of the hospital, which led the War Office to repeatedly ask searching questions of the clinicians, managers and superintendents of many of the numerous hospitals that were mobilised for the treatment of shell shocked veterans between 1914 and 1918, and to frequently demand evidence that they were getting value for money.

So, if you have read this far, then I am confident that as you read on you will certainly get value for your money. Professor Kelly has produced a fascinating account not just of the short history of the Richmond War Hospital, but also an introduction to the ever-fascinating problem of shell shock, and glimpses into the lives and backgrounds of those who found themselves within the walls of the Richmond War Hospital, whether as patients or clinicians.

Professor Sir Simon Wessely
President, Royal College of Psychiatrists

# Preface

By any standard, this is an absolutely facsinating book. It concerns the story of the Richmond War Hospital, which was set up during a turbulent political period in this country, in 1916, and remained open until 1919. A small number of beds were set aside in the greater Richmond mental asylum to deal with 'shell shock' cases arising from the First World War. The unit was quite separate from the rest of the hospital, and the recovery rate was surprisingly positive compared to the dismal clinical picture in the rest of the large mental asylums at that time. The history of shell shock has had a long, confusing struggle to see the light of day, and it is only in recent years that it has finally been accepted as a genuine traumatic reality, under the heading of PTSD (post-traumatic stress disorder).

Professor Brendan Kelly is a highly qualified psychiatrist and experienced clinician, but I suspect that his deeper passion is for history. Had he chosen a different path, he might well have ended up as a major historian. This comes across in the clear, simple style in which he writes. Also, he is careful to avoid the mistake, which as a clinician he might well have done, of putting his own interpretation, or offering a critique, as to the relevence of this unit in the wider development of psychiatric services. No, he sticks to his last as a historian and simply gives the facts, with a number of illuminating case illustrations of what happened in the day-to-day running of the unit. He quotes, in the language of the time, the comments of various authorities who were involved with the unit at that time, and later. Thus he leaves it to the reader to make up his or her own mind about the relevence of all this. This makes the whole book so much more valuable than it might otherwise have been.

Anyone with even a passing interest in history, or in psychiatry, will be enthralled by this concise, meticulously-reserched and utterly engrossing book. Once you take it up, you will be unable to put it down, and find yourself reading it right through to the last page.

Professor Kelly is to be congratulated for providing us with such a valuable insight into one of the largely neglected chapters in the history of mental health services in Ireland and elsewhere.

Professor Ivor Browne
Emeritus Professor of Psychiatry
University College Dublin

# Introduction

In late 1918, a 37-year old, single, Roman Catholic gunner in the British army, Gunner KL, was admitted to the Richmond War Hospital, a 32-bed establishment on the grounds of the Richmond District Asylum in Dublin, dedicated to the treatment of soldiers with mental troubles as a result of the First World War (1914–18).[1]

According to archival clinical records, Gunner KL's left arm was 'badly torn. Black slough on top of elbow. Several patches of skin torn off the arm, which is septic'. Mentally, Gunner KL was 'rather irritable and complains of feeling nervous and of severe pain at the back of his head, and also of noises, dreams and night-terrors. States he can see shells bursting about and he states he wakes up very frightened at night.'

Prior to his admission to the Richmond War Hospital, Gunner KL had been in another Dublin hospital, but suffered from memory problems while on leave into town: 'He remembers being in town and only remembers getting as far as Parkgate Street on his return journey.... The rest seems a blank to him.' This episode, allied with his nervousness, hallucinations ('noises') and night-terrors, precipitated Gunner KL's admission to the Richmond War Hospital for the assessment and management of the psychological consequences of war.

Gunner KL had joined the army in 1914 and served in France from 1915 to 1918. In 1917, he was 'blown up and rendered unconscious in Passendael Ridge' (at Passchendaele in Belgium, site of the Third Battle of Ypres, from July to November 1917). The following year, Gunner KL 'was wounded in the right mastoid region [at the side of his head, behind his right ear] by a splinter of a shell', and two months later was sent home, a case of 'shell shock'.[2]

On his first night in the Richmond War Hospital in 1918, Gunner KL 'remained quiet and slept fairly well'. One week after admission, medical notes record that he was 'feeling much better and is fairly bright and cheerful. His arm is much improved.... Eats and sleeps well'. Two weeks after admission, Gunner KL was 'very quiet and well-conducted and gives no trouble. He is fairly bright and cheerful. His arm is very much better'. Clearly, the quietude and medical care on offer at the War Hospital had benefitted Gunner KL both mentally and physically.

Four weeks after admission, Gunner KL 'was given three days leave to go home to attend his mother's funeral.... He returned punctually. He is very quiet and is well-conducted and gives no trouble. His arm is now about healed. Eats and sleeps well'. The improvement was sustained the following week, at which point Gunner KL was not only 'very quiet and well-conducted' but also 'quite rational in his conversation'. Several weeks later, Gunner KL was discharged from the War Hospital, relieved of his symptoms – at least for now.

The case of Gunner KL is typical of many who were treated at the Richmond War Hospital between 16 June 1916 and 23 December 1919. Over this period, the War Hospital attended to the needs of 362 soldiers with nervous and mental troubles as a result of the First World War. Gunner KL's apparently rapid recovery was by no means unique: more than half of the soldiers admitted reportedly recovered following their time there,[3] although a significant minority moved on to different locations for further treatment (for example, Belfast War Hospital), and a small number were transferred to general asylums.

Sergeant RS, for example, a 20-year-old, single, Church of England sergeant, was admitted to the Richmond War Hospital in early 1919. On admission, Sergeant RS was 'silent and morose in his manner and inclined to be uncommunicative. He hesitates before replying to my questions. He complains of headache – bad one day, well another; of the blood rushing to the top of his head and down again; of noises ringing in his head; and of voices which he cannot recognise. He seems very upset but tries to preserve a calm exterior. He seems depressed'.

Sergeant RS had joined the army in 1916 and went to the front in 1917. He was taken prisoner at Vandeuil (in northeastern France) and spent eight months as a prisoner of war: 'He states he felt queer in the prison camp on one occasion'. Following his return to England, Sergeant RS went home to the West of Ireland but was later admitted to King George V Hospital (a military hospital in Dublin) from which he was transferred to the Richmond War Hospital for management of psychological symptoms.

On his first night at the Richmond War Hospital, Sergeant RS 'remained quiet and slept well during the night'. One week after admission, Sergeant RS remained 'very silent and defiant in his manner. He makes little freedom with anyone. He sometimes runs downstairs as if in response to a call and seems rather disappointed when he finds it was not so. He admits he hears voices but is inclined to make light of the matter and says they are now much less troublesome. Sleeps and eats well'.

Two weeks after admission, Sergeant RS was 'looking much better physically but mentally the improvement is slight. He admits he hears voices but remarks they are less troublesome. He is very distant and does not relish my questions. He is very quiet. Sleeps and eats well'. One month after admission, Sergeant RS remained 'sullen and morose in his manner, being distant and uncommunicative. He used threats towards the attendant the other day, saying he would put his teeth down his neck. When I spoke to him about it he was very annoyed and told me I wanted him to say what was being done on him but that no power on earth would make him tell it. He evidently imagines some form of persecution is employed against him. He still hears voices. Sleeps and eats well'.

Two months after admission, Sergeant RS was 'still sullen and very distant. He entertains persecutory delusions [paranoid beliefs without basis] and is subject to hallucinations of hearing [hearing things that are not present]. He is, however, quiet. He sleeps and eats well'. Three weeks later, after almost three months in the Richmond War Hospital, Sergeant RS was 'transferred to Belfast War Hospital' (which had opened in 1917)[4] for further treatment of what appears to be both the psychological effects of war and a possibly unrelated episode of mental illness.

In diagnosing and managing cases such as Gunner KL and Sergeant RS, the Richmond War Hospital represented a unique and ground-breaking initiative in Irish mental health services during an era when the Irish asylums were constantly expanding,[5] and there were deep concerns about conditions and treatments in many of them,[6] including the main Richmond Asylum itself.[7] The Richmond War Hospital differed significantly from the main asylum, however, because it was aimed at a specific population (soldiers), did not require that patients be formally certified as insane, and assumed a more progressive approach to treatment and recovery. While many of these changes were apparently short-lived, and did not immediately generalise to

Ireland's broader asylum system after the War Hospital closed in 1919, they were nonetheless provocative changes which would echo through later reforms of Ireland's psychiatric hospitals throughout the 1900s.[8]

This book explores the history of the Richmond War Hospital both in the context of the Irish asylum system of the 1800s and 1900s, and in the context of the network of war hospitals established throughout the United Kingdom of Great Britain and Ireland during the First World War. As a result, this book examines the history of the Richmond War Hospital from one particular perspective, that of *medical* history, and focuses especially on the War Hospital's place in the history of Ireland's asylum system and, as the title suggests, shell shock and its treatment at the War Hospital.

This book argues that the Richmond War Hospital served as an exemplar of many of the reforms that were sorely needed in the Irish asylum system in the early 1900s and, as a result, this book places greatest emphasis on the Richmond War Hospital in the context of the Richmond District Asylum and the broader Irish asylum system, rather than as part of the broader network of war hospitals. On this basis, the book explores the Richmond District Asylum prior to the arrival of the War Hospital and again after its closure, arguing that the Richmond War Hospital was more than simply a place where soldiers were treated for nervous problems, but was also an important harbinger of much-needed reform of the Irish asylums.

Chapter One sets the historical scene by exploring the history of the Richmond District Asylum from the time of its opening in 1814 to the arrival of the War Hospital in 1916. This chapter documents the rather bleak situation pertaining to mental health care in early nineteenth century Ireland and then focuses on the changes and reforms introduced at the Richmond Asylum throughout the 1800s. During this period, there were considerable innovations at the asylum, coupled, paradoxically, with an apparently inexorable rise in patient numbers. Taken together, these two factors made the Richmond the obvious choice when establishing a psychiatric war hospital in Ireland in 1916.

Chapter Two explores the foundation of the Richmond War Hospital in June 1916 and looks at the role of the Easter Rising (April 1916) in establishing the diagnosis of 'shock' at the Richmond prior to the arrival of the War Hospital, with its cases of 'shell shock' later that year. This chapter also explores case-histories of traumatised soldiers drawn from the archives of the Richmond War Hospital, presented and discussed in order to illustrate key themes and developments at the hospital.

Chapter Three looks at diagnostic practices at the Richmond War Hospital, commencing with an exploration of the more general emergence of the diagnosis of shell shock during the First World War. This is followed by an examination of diagnostic and clinical practices at the Richmond War Hospital, illustrated by further exploration of clinical case histories from its archives. These case histories are discussed in the context of broader diagnostic practices among soldiers treated at war hospitals for psychological and nervous problems associated with the war.

Chapter Four examines treatments at the Richmond War Hospital, and explores both treatments provided for the psychological effects of the war and challenges presented by physical illnesses, such as malaria and epilepsy. Again, these themes are explored though examination of case histories drawn from the archives of the Richmond War Hospital, up until its closure on 23 December 1919.

Chapter Five looks at developments at the Richmond District Asylum following the closure of the War Hospital in 1919 up to the early 2000s, when, after 200 years of mental health care on the site, the era of the large asylum at Grangegorman came to an end. In 2013, the old inpatient hospital was replaced by a network of community resources operated by multi-disciplinary mental health teams, augmented by inpatient facilities. This chapter examines these developments with particular focus on the place of the Richmond War Hospital in the multi-layered history of the Grangegorman campus, and the treatments likely received by the minority of soldiers who were transferred from the Richmond War Hospital to the general asylum system.

To conclude, Chapter Six examines the enduring legacy of the Richmond War Hospital. This chapter draws together the story of the War Hospital in the context of the Irish asylum system and in the context of efforts to treat soldiers traumatised by the First World War in various war hospitals throughout Ireland and Great Britain.

Overall, the Richmond War Hospital was a complex institution that not only reported a high recovery rate but also pointed the way for future reform of Ireland's asylum system, helped (with the other war hospitals) to bring positive changes to the practice of psychiatry throughout Great Britain and Ireland, and can also help deepen Ireland's memory of the psychological effects of the First World War on the Irish.

While the mechanics of warfare may have changed significantly in the 100 years since the Richmond War Hospital opened, its story remains highly relevant, not least because many soldiers today still develop disabling psychiatric symptoms when exposed to conflict. And even now, relieving their distress can sometimes seem just as challenging as it was a century ago, at the Richmond.

## A Note on Terminology

Throughout this book, original language and terminology from the 1700s, 1800s and 1900s have been maintained. This represents an attempt to optimise fidelity to historical sources and does not represent an endorsement of the broader use of such terminology in contemporary settings.

## Endnotes

[1] All case histories in this book are drawn from: Richmond War Hospital Case Book (1918-1919), National Archives of Ireland, Bishop Street, Dublin 8 (BR/PRIV 1223 Richmond War). The names, regiments, precise admission dates and other identifying details relating to the soldiers are not presented, in order to preserve anonymity. The programme of research upon which this book is based was approved by the Ethics Committee of the Health Service Executive, Dublin North City, Ireland.

[2] Myers, C.S., 'A contribution to the study of shell shock'. *Lancet* 1915; 185: 316-20; Myers, C.S., 'Contributions to the study of shell shock: Being an account of certain disorders of cutaneous sensibility'. *Lancet* 1916; 187: 608-13; Rivers, W.H.R., *Instinct and the Unconscious: A Contribution to a Biological Theory of the Psycho-Neuroses*. Cambridge: Cambridge University Press, 1920; Shepherd, B., *A War of Nerves: Soldiers and Psychiatrists, 1914-1994*. London: Pimlico, 2002.

[3] Reynolds, J. *Grangegorman: Psychiatric Care in Dublin since 1815*. Dublin: Institute of Public Administration in association with Eastern Health Board, 1992; pp. 217-9.

[4] Dawson, W.R., 'The work of the Belfast War Hospital (1917-1919)'. *Journal of Mental Science* 1925; 71: 219-24.

[5] Kelly, B.D., 'Mental Health Law in Ireland, 1821-1902: Building the Asylums'. *Medico-Legal Journal* 2008; 76: 19-25; Kelly, B.D., 'Mental Health Law in Ireland, 1821-1902: Dealing with the "increase of insanity in Ireland"'. *Medico-Legal Journal* 2008; 76: 26-33.

[6] Finnane, P., *Insanity and the Insane in Post-Famine Ireland*. London: Croom Helm, 1981.

[7] Kelly, B.D., 'One hundred years ago: The Richmond Asylum, Dublin in 1907'. *Irish Journal of Psychological Medicine* 2007; 24: 108–14.

[8] Kelly, B.D., 'Mental health law in Ireland, 1945 to 2001: Reformation and renewal'. *Medico-Legal Journal* 2008; 76: 65-72.

# 1

# The Richmond Asylum, 1814–1916

The Richmond War Hospital (1916-19) formed part of one of Ireland's oldest and best-known psychiatric institutions, the Richmond Asylum in Grangegorman, Dublin. This chapter explores the history of the Richmond Asylum prior to the establishment of the Richmond War Hospital in 1916, and sets out the context in which the War Hospital came into being and operated.

When examining the recorded history of the Richmond Asylum and, indeed, Ireland's other psychiatric institutions, one could easily conclude that Ireland's asylums were solely a mechanism of social control, designed to warehouse the mentally ill, intellectually disabled, and other individuals who simply did not fit in, with little emphasis on the treatment and amelioration of mental illness.

This impression stems primarily from the fact that much of the history of mental health care in Ireland focuses on the emergence of Ireland's asylums as *institutions*,[1] as evidenced by detailed and excellent histories of specific hospitals such as St Patrick's Hospital, Dublin,[2] Our Lady's Hospital, Cork,[3] the Richmond District Asylum (Grangegorman Mental Hospital, St Brendan's Hospital) Dublin,[4] St Vincent's Hospital, Fairview, Dublin,[5] Bloomfield Hospital, Dublin[6] and Holywell Hospital, Belfast.[7] The literature has also, to a lesser but still significant

1

extent, focussed on the history of mental health legislation, chiefly as a result of laws permitting detention on the grounds of mental disorder[8] and the fact that Ireland's programme of psychiatric institutions[9] found its roots in continual revisions of mental health legislation throughout the 1800s and early 1900s.[10]

These are both important topics – the establishment of asylums and the law – but an exclusive focus on these topics accords insufficient importance to the experiences of individual patients within the Irish asylum system. How did these patients end up in there? What alternatives were available for them and their families at the time? What was life like in the asylums? What treatments, if any were offered? Did the treatments work? And where does the Richmond War Hospital fit into the story of the patients who inhabited Ireland's extraordinary network of asylums?

This chapter, by way of background to the Richmond War Hospital, focuses on the Richmond Asylum in the century before the War Hospital was established there: What treatments were offered to the inpatients in the Richmond throughout the 1800s and early 1900s? Did these treatments help? How did these treatments and practices set the scene for the treatments and policies of the War Hospital when it opened in 1916?

## Mental Health Care in Nineteenth Century Ireland

To understand the Richmond Asylum it is first necessary to understand the context in which the asylum developed, and the needs it sought to meet. In Ireland, there was scant provision for individuals with mental disorder throughout the seventeenth and eighteenth centuries.[11] As a result, the mentally ill tended towards lives of vagrancy and destitution.[12] In 1817, the House of Commons of the United Kingdom of Great Britain and Ireland established a committee to investigate the plight of the mentally ill in Ireland. The committee reported a disturbing picture:

> When a strong man or woman gets the complaint [mental disorder], the only way they have to manage is by making a hole in the floor of the cabin, not high enough for the person to stand up in, with a crib over it to prevent his getting up. This hole is about five feet deep, and they give this wretched being his food there, and there he generally dies.[13]

Notwithstanding this rather bleak situation, the 1700s saw some early signs of change. In Dublin, St Patrick's Hospital was founded in 1747 following the benevolent bequest of Jonathan Swift (1667-1745), satirist, writer and Dean of St Patrick's Cathedral. St Patrick's Hospital was a private, charitable institution, aimed at providing high quality care to a finite number of individuals, without the broader, population-level responsibilities of government-run institutions.[14] Despite this focus on individual patient care, however, even a dedicated history of St Patrick's, replete with minute detail about the estate, the building and other aspects of the *institution*, finds that the patients themselves are remarkably elusive: insofar as the patient experience is mentioned in the records, most of the attention is paid to administrative rather clinical matters.[15]

There were some other early advances in providing for the mentally ill outside of Dublin, most notably in Cork, where a pioneering psychiatrist, Dr William Saunders Hallaran, founded a public asylum in 1791, to accommodate 24 patients. By 1822, Cork Lunatic Asylum had expanded to cater for over 300 patients.[16] In 1810, Hallaran went on to publish Ireland's first textbook of psychiatry, *An Enquiry into the Causes producing the Extraordinary Addition to the Number of Insane together with*

*Extended Observations on the Cure of Insanity with Hints as to the Better Management of Public Asylums for Insane Persons.*[17]

In his authoritative history of medicine in Ireland, Fleetwood notes that Hallaran at least made a real effort at active treatment of the mentally ill.[18] In fact, Hallaran brought unprecedented critical rigour to the evaluation of treatments for, and causes of, mental illness, through both his academic writings and his critical clinical practice.[19] Blood-letting, for example, was commonly performed in psychiatric settings throughout the 1700s, and often involved leeches,[20] but Hallaran wrote that blood-letting 'to any great extent does not often seem to be desirable, and except in recent cases, does not even appear to be admissible'.[21] This unconventional view was soon shared by other prominent psychiatrists including Dr Philippe Pinel (1745-1826) at the Hospice de la Salpêtrière in Paris.[22]

Hallaran was also doubtful about emetics (to induce vomiting) and purgatives,[23] even as this placed him at odds with such prominent physicians as Dr Martin Tuomy of the Royal College of Physicians of Ireland, in his 1810 *Treatise on the Principal Diseases of Dublin.*[24] Hallaran was similarly independent-minded in relation to the use of digitalis, opium, camphor,[25] and, especially, mercury, despite the latter's established use for syphilis[26] and neuro-syphilis[27] – disorders which, a full century later, would present substantial challenges to the war hospitals of the First World War.[28] Again, Hallaran's prescient doubts were borne out as the nineteenth century progressed and mercury declined in popularity.[29]

From an even broader, international, historical perspective, there are similarities between the generally humanitarian approach of Hallaran in Cork and those of Pinel in Paris, who pioneered less custodial approaches to asylum care,[30] and William Tuke (1732–1822), an English Quaker businessman who founded the York Retreat in 1796, based on policies of care and gentleness, as well as medical supervision.[31] While this humane approach was much needed in nineteenth century Ireland owing to a history of under-provision for the mentally ill,[32] and would later be echoed in the Richmond War Hospital,[33] Hallaran's therapeutic and institutional enthusiasms clearly supported 'the extraordinary addition to the number of insane' committed to Irish asylums throughout the 1800s[34] – a trend which, ironically, would later cause Hallaran profound concern.[35]

Notwithstanding this unintended effect of his therapeutic enthusiasm, this evidence of Hallaran's critical engagement with a range of therapies for mental illness helps redress the literature's overwhelming focus on another aspect of Hallaran's practice: his enthusiasm for the 'circulating swing',[36] originally described by Dr Joseph Mason Cox (1763–1818), a Scottish psychiatrist and author of *Practical Observations on Insanity*.[37] Cox described a 'rotative couch' aimed at inducing sleep and treating mania.[38] Cox advised suspending a chair from the ceiling using ropes; seating the patient securely in the chair; and then instructing an asylum attendant to rotate the chair at a given speed, thus spinning the patient around a vertical axis for a given period of time.[39] This rather alarming technique was used at many asylums throughout nineteenth century Europe, especially in German-speaking countries.[40]

In Cork, Hallaran assembled a similar apparatus which, in the 'obstinate and furious', generated 'a sufficiency of alarm to insure obedience' and, in the 'melancholic', 'a natural interest in the affairs of life'.[41] Predictably, Hallaran's enthusiasm for the 'circulating swing', which would clearly violate contemporary human rights standards,[42] has substantially over-shadowed his other contributions to the development of mental health services in Ireland, most notably his critical engagement with contemporary treatments for mental disorder in the first edition of his textbook[43] and his careful engagement with apparent causes of mental disorder in the second.[44]

Most of all, however, Hallaran's work underlines the point that the history of psychiatry is, in large part, a history of therapeutic enthusiasm, with all of the triumphs, tragedies and hubris that such enthusiasm brings. While Hallaran's careful consideration of the effectiveness of traditional treatments was greatly to be welcomed, there can be little doubt that his altruistic desire to accommodate the 'hurried weight of human calamity'[45] demonstrates the role of therapeutic enthusiasm in increasing committal rates.[46] Over a century later, renewed therapeutic enthusiasm was to contribute significantly to the establishment of the Richmond War Hospital, although on that occasion the practices and treatments it engendered appeared substantially more benign (Chapter Four).[47]

In any case, in the century leading up to the establishment of the Richmond War Hospital, asylum admission rates continued to rise in Ireland, compounded by intensive legislative activity and the establishment of a large network of asylums across the country: in 1851 there were 3,234 individuals in the Irish asylums and by 1891 this had increased to 11,265.[48] From a therapeutic perspective, Hallaran's disillusionment with certain physical treatments was to become widely shared during this period, leading to the emergence of a new therapeutic enthusiasm, this time for a concept commonly known as 'moral management'.[49] This was the paradigm that underpinned much of the thinking behind the new asylums of the 1800s[50] including, most notably, the Richmond Asylum in Dublin, which accepted its first patient in 1814,[51] four years after Hallaran's seminal textbook appeared[52] and over a century before the Richmond War Hospital was established there.

## The Richmond Asylum in the 1800s

Like the majority of the psychiatric hospitals that emerged in Ireland during the nineteenth century, the Richmond Asylum was a large, complicated institution that attempted to perform a difficult task: caring for the mentally ill in a complex and often unwelcoming society.[53]

In Ireland, the Richmond Asylum was at the forefront of *both* therapeutic enthusiasm and efforts to reform mental health care, in order to provide better care and accommodation for the mentally ill. From the early 1800s, the Dublin establishment pioneered 'moral treatment' in Ireland. Dr Jean-Étienne Dominique Esquirol (1772–1840), a French doctor, defined moral treatment as 'the application of the faculty of intelligence and of emotions in the treatment of mental alienation.'[54] The moral management approach represented a significant break from the past which had emphasised custodial care rather than engagement with each patient as an individual. Today, such an approach might well be described as 'milieu therapy' involving a group-based approach to recovery and establishment of therapeutic communities.[55]

One of the key benefits of the moral management approach was that it represented a significant move away from traditional treatments such as blood-letting, routine confinement and restraint. Diet, exercise and occupation were emphasised. To underline this approach, the Richmond was run chiefly by moral governors during the first half of the nineteenth century; these included Richard Grace (1815-30) and Samuel Wrigley (1831-57), separated by a brief interlude during which Dr William Heise (1830-31) ran the establishment.

In 1846, over three decades after it opened, the Inspector of Lunatic Asylums reported very positively on the Richmond:

I have been in the habit of visiting this institution frequently during the last year, and of inspecting it very minutely, and have also had the pleasure of attending the Board of Governors on various occasions. It is unnecessary for me to add, that the general business is most satisfactorily performed.... The Asylum continues to maintain its high character as being one of the best-managed institutions in the country; and also for the great order, regularity, and state of cleanliness in which it is kept. The beds and bedding are kept always very clean.[56]

Notwithstanding these high standards, the Inspector, Dr Francis White, felt it was 'necessary to enlarge the Richmond Asylum by the addition of a wing to accommodate 100 patients, and also of an infirmary, so that the Asylum, when enlarged, may altogether be adequate to the accommodation of 400'.[57]

Five years later, in 1851, the *Census of Ireland* presented a detailed *'Report upon the number and conditions of lunatics and idiots'* throughout Ireland and recorded that there were now 278 inpatients (132 male, 146 female) in the Richmond. The report recorded that the 'industrial pursuits and amusements provided' for males at the Richmond included 'gardening, weaving, mat-making, shoemaking, carpenters' work, drafts and other amusements'.[58] For females, pursuits included 'needle-work, knitting, fancy work, reading, writing, music and dancing'.

All of this activity was consistent with the moral management paradigm that was still in evidence in the Richmond and which would later be echoed in the therapeutic approach of the War Hospital in the early 1900s.

In the mid-1800s, as this approach was still evolving, one of its logical developments was the use education as a means of treating mental disorder, and this was duly pioneered at the

Richmond by Dr Joseph Lalor, Resident Medical Superintendent (RMS) from 1857 to 1886:

> I consider that education and training are most valuable
> agents in the treatment ... and that it expresses in name
> and substance what has long been known in reference to
> lunatics in general as to their moral treatment...starting
> with the proposition that education and training form the
> basis of the moral treatment of all classes of the insane.[59]

Under Lalor, the school at the Richmond soon became a
central element in hospital life, and subjects taught included
reading, writing, arithmetic, geometry, algebra, geography,
drawing, needlework and various other arts and crafts.[60] Pro-
fessional teachers were employed and the National Board of
Education recognised the classes in 1862. Dr Daniel Hack Tuke
(1827-95) wrote approvingly of the Richmond schools in the
influential *Journal of Mental Science*:

> To myself, the schools which are in active operation there
> under Dr Lalor were of deep interest, and I venture to
> think that some useful hints may be gathered from what
> we witnessed on the occasion. Indeed so valuable did the
> system pursued appear to me to be, that I stayed another
> day in Dublin in order to see more of the working of the
> schools.... The pupils are divided into three classes on both
> sides of the house, there being three male and three female
> trained teachers.... The patients stood in circles marked
> out by a chalk line, presenting a very orderly appearance,
> while the teacher asked them questions on geography, &c.,
> or gave them an object lesson. While of course there was a
> great difference in the expression of those who were being
> taught, and in their responsiveness to the questions put to
> them, there was a general air not only of propriety but of
> interestedness which was very striking. Some, in fact, were
> extremely bright and lively....[61]

Following Lalor's death, his obituary in the *Journal of Mental Science* described him as 'excellent and kind-hearted' and drew attention to his achievements with the school at the Richmond:[62]

> It is stated on good authority that [prior to Lalor's appointment to the Richmond] refractory patients were confined in cells for most of the day as well as the night, receiving their food in such a way as best suited the convenience of the attendants. Open-air exercise was rarely permitted, and then only in the dark confined yards or sheds surrounded by stone walls. All this was changed by Dr Lalor; better grounds were prepared, games were introduced, and the general comfort of the patients was attended to. Dr Lalor, as is well known, enthusiastically carried out the school system....

> It should be stated that for two years before he became Superintendent a school had been in operation on the female side under an excellent school mistress. It was Dr Lalor who introduced the same system for the male patients, and he obtained additional teachers, trained under the National Board, for the female school. Singing and music were much cultivated, while object and picture lessons were given, as well as others in natural history and geography. At the Exhibition held some years ago in Dublin, drawings, paintings, and industrial work, all executed by the patients, attracted considerable attention. Along with the schools, concerts were given every fortnight, or even weekly....

The *Irish Times* referred to Lalor's 'undoubted genius' and paid tribute to 'the human projects which he both conceived and put into execution, with a decision of character and a perseverance absolutely necessary in one holding his position. In this respect he had the strength of mind and the will of a Lesseps'.[63] Ferdinand Marie, Vicomte de Lesseps (1805–94), was a French diplomat who devoted enormous time and energy to developing the Suez Canal, which opened in 1869 after some ten years of construction work; in the 1800s, reforming an asylum was considered to be a task of similar magnitude, and it was one at which Lalor clearly excelled.

Despite the determined and progressive steps taken at the Richmond by Lalor and others, however, the number of psychiatric inpatients continued to rise inexorably during the nineteenth century and, by1892, the Richmond's problems had increased greatly, owing chiefly to overcrowding. The Inspector of Lunatics became increasingly alarmed:

> During the year no relief has been obtained as regards the overcrowding of this asylum. The number of patients now almost reaches 1500, whereas the asylum only accommodates about 1100. It is therefore not to be wondered at that the general health of the institution is far from satisfactory, and that the death-rate, as compared with other Irish asylums, is high, amounting to 12.5%, the average death-rate in a similar institution in this country being 8.3%. Constant outbreaks of zymotic disease [acute infectious diseases] have occurred. Dysentery has for many years past been almost endemic in this institution - 73 cases with 14 deaths occurred last year, and it may be mentioned that in no less than three of these cases secondary abscesses were found in the liver.[64]

The 'death rate' of 8.3 per cent in Irish district asylums was derived by dividing the number of deaths in Irish district asylums in 1892 (995 deaths) by the daily average number of asylum residents; on 1 January 1893, that number stood at 12,133. Of those who died in district asylums, almost 20 per cent underwent post-mortem examinations which, in the opinion of the Inspector, were 'of so much importance for the protection of the insane and for the furtherance of the scientific study of insanity.'[65]

The higher death rate at the Richmond (12.5 per cent) was possibly related to particular problems with overcrowding and infective illnesses there.[66] Comparable death rates were, however, reported in other jurisdictions,[67] with, for example, a 14 per cent death rate in South Carolina Lunatic Asylum between 1890 and 1915.[68] In Canada, 33 per cent of men and 21 per cent of women admitted to the Toronto Asylum between 1851 and 1891 died there.[69]

In Ireland, too, these kinds of problems, especially those related to overcrowding, were by no means limited to the Richmond. In 1893, the Inspector expressed alarm at 'the great increase of lunacy which has taken place of late years in this country' generally:[70]

> The accommodation in District Asylums in this country still continues quite inadequate to supply the wants of the insane population. We have again to repeat the statement made in former reports that the overcrowding is rapidly increasing, and that the necessity for further accommodation is becoming more and more urgent.[71]

Perhaps the most interesting feature of the Inspector's report in 1893 was that, similarly to previous years, there was minimal mention of specific *treatments* provided for mental disorder in the various asylums, including the Richmond. The report on the Richmond contained considerable detail about many other matters, including physical illnesses ('consumption', 'pneumonia', 'heart disease'), accidents ('fracture of skull, ending fatally, resulting from blows inflicted by another patient'), attendance at 'divine service', and 'precautions as regards stores' (primarily to prevent theft).[72] Specific *treatments*, however, did not feature in the report to any significant extent, although there was considerable detail about diet:

The dietary has been improved by the substitution of soup for coffee on Wednesdays, and will now compare favourably with the scale in use in other similar institutions. The patients get beef, potatoes and soup for dinner on Sunday, Monday, Tuesday and Saturday, and pork on Thursday. Perhaps the Governers might sanction the use of mutton on one day of the week, so as to afford greater variety in the food. Tea and bread is given for breakfast, and cocoa in the evening. The meals are served with as great regularity and order as the overcrowded state of the halls permit. Delf is in use for the service of each meal.[73]

## Moving Towards the Twentieth Century

In 1886, three decades before the arrival of the War Hospital, the Richmond acquired a new RMS, the pioneering Dr John Conolly Norman (1853–1908), who stayed in post until his sudden death in 1908. Among the many changes Norman brought to the hospital were changes in the medical staff, most notably though the promotion of Dr Eleonora Fleury (1867–1960). Fleury was a remarkable figure who attained first class honours as the first female medical graduate of the Royal University of Ireland in 1890 and a gold medal for her MD degree in 1893. In 1894, at the suggestion of Norman, she became the first female member of the Medico Psychological Association of Great Britain and Ireland (MPA) and, thus, the first female psychiatrist in Ireland or Great Britain. Fleury worked at both the Richmond and St Ita's Hospital in Portrane and was also highly politically active in the Irish Republican cause, resulting in her eventual imprisonment.[74]

In 1907, when the Richmond's population had reached some 1,600 patients, Norman suggested that perhaps the increase in Ireland's asylum population seen during the 1800s had finally peaked. Uncharacteristically, Norman was wrong: the numbers in Irish asylums continued to increase until the late

1950s, at which time there were over 20,000 psychiatric inpatients in Ireland. As a result, the early decades of the 1900s saw increased pressure on asylums to address the problems presented by overcrowding, and this concern was soon translated into enthusiasm for new forms of treatment including malarial therapy, insulin coma therapy, psycho-surgery and convulsive treatment, all of which were introduced at the Richmond in the early to mid-1900s (see Chapter Five).

In 1908, however, just eight years before the War Hospital was established there, the Richmond appointed another new RMS, Dr John O'Conor Donelan, who stayed in post until 1937. This was an especially tumultuous period in Irish history with the occurrences of the Easter Rising (1916), War of Independence (1919–21) and Civil War (1922–23). Fleury was very politically active throughout these events, resulting in her inevitable imprisonment in Kilmainham Gaol in Dublin in 1923.[75] Political activism among staff was not, however, the only dramatic development at the Richmond during this period, as, in 1916, the Richmond War Hospital opened its doors, starting new chapters in the eventful history of the Richmond and the colourful, occasionally disturbing, history of psychiatry in Ireland.

### Endnotes

[1] The emergence of Ireland's psychiatric institutions has dominated Irish psychiatric history to date owing, most likely, to the remarkable size of the institutions, and their complex legacy.

[2] Malcolm, E., *Swift's Hospital: A History of St Patrick's Hospital, Dublin, 1746-1989*. Dublin: Gill and Macmillan, 1989; Clare, A.W., 'St. Patrick's Hospital'. *American Journal of Psychiatry* 1998; 155: 1599.

[3] Henry, H.M., *Our Lady's Hospital, Cork: History of the Mental Hospital in Cork Spanning 200 years*. Cork: Haven Books, 1989.

[4] Reynolds, J., *Grangegorman: Psychiatric Care in Dublin since 1815*.

Dublin: Institute of Public Administration in association with Eastern Health Board, 1992.

5 Collins, A., *St Vincent's Hospital, Fairview: An Illustrated history, 1857-2007*. Dublin: Albertine Kennedy Publishing with Duke Kennedy Sweetman, 2007.

6 Douglas, G., Goodbody, R., Mauger, A., Davey, J., *Bloomfield: A History, 1812-2012*. Dublin: Ashfield Press, 2012.

7 Mulholland, M., *To Comfort Always: A History of Holywell Hospital, 1898-1998*. Ballymena: Homefirst Community Trust, 1998.

8 McAuley, F., *Insanity, Psychiatry and Criminal Responsibility*. Dublin: Round Hall Press, 1993; Cooney, T., O'Neill, O., *Psychiatric Detention: Civil Commitment in Ireland* (Kritik 1). Wicklow: Baikonur, 1996; Gibbons, P., Mulryan, N., O'Connor, A., 'Guilty but insane: The insanity defence in Ireland, 1850–1995'. *British Journal of Psychiatry* 1997; 170: 467-72; Prior, P., 'Prisoner or lunatic? The official debate on the criminal lunatic in nineteenth-century Ireland'. *History of Psychiatry* 2004; 15: 177–92; Kelly, B.D., 'The Mental Treatment Act 1945 in Ireland: An historical enquiry'. *History of Psychiatry* 2008; 19: 47-67.

9 Finnane, P., *Insanity and the Insane in Post-Famine Ireland*. London: Croom Helm, 1981; Reuber, M., 'The architecture of psychological management: The Irish asylums (1801-1922)'. *Psychological Medicine* 1996; 26: 1179–89; Reuber, M., 'Moral management and the 'unseen eye': Public lunatic asylums in Ireland, 1800–1845'. In: Malcolm, E., Jones, G. (eds) *Medicine, Disease and the State in Ireland, 1650-1940* (pp. 208–33). Cork: Cork University Press, 1999.

10 Kelly, B.D., 'Mental Health Law in Ireland, 1821-1902: Building the Asylums'. *Medico-Legal Journal* 2008; 76: 19-25; Kelly, B.D., 'Mental Health Law in Ireland, 1821-1902: Dealing with the 'increase of insanity in Ireland'. *Medico-Legal Journal* 2008; 76: 26-33; Kelly, B.D., 'Mental health law in Ireland, 1945 to 2001: Reformation and renewal'. *Medico-Legal Journal* 2008; 76: 65-72.

11 Psychiatrist. 'Insanity in Ireland'. *The Bell* 1944; 7: 303-10; Robins, J. *Fools and Mad: A History of the Insane in Ireland*. Dublin: Institute of Public Administration, 1986; Bartlett, P., *The Poor Law of Lunacy*. London and Washington: Leicester University Press, 1999.

[12] Finnane, P., *Insanity and the Insane in Post-Famine Ireland*. London: Croom Helm, 1981.

[13] Shorter, E., *A History of Psychiatry: From the Era of the Asylum to the Age of Prozac*. New York: John Wiley and Sons, 1997 (quoted on pp. 1-2).

[14] Clare, A.W., 'St. Patrick's Hospital'. *American Journal of Psychiatry* 1998; 155: 1599.

[15] Malcolm, *Swift's Hospital*.

[16] Robins, J., *Fools and Mad: A History of the Insane in Ireland*. Dublin: Institute of Public Administration, 1986.

[17] Hallaran, W.S., *An Enquiry into the Causes Producing the Extraordinary Addition to the Number of Insane together with Extended Observations on the Cure of Insanity with Hints as to the Better Management of Public Asylums for Insane Persons*. Cork: Edwards and Savage, 1810.

[18] Fleetwood, J.F., *The History of Medicine in Ireland* (Second Edition). Dublin: Skellig Press, 1983; p. 172.

[19] Kelly, B.D., 'Dr William Saunders Hallaran and psychiatric practice in nineteenth-century Ireland'. *Irish Journal of Medical Science* 2008; 177: 79-84.

[20] Farmar, T., *Patients, Potions and Physicians: A Social History of Medicine in Ireland*. Dublin: A & A Farmar in association with the Royal College of Physicians of Ireland, 2004.

[21] Hallaran, *An Enquiry*, p. 50.

[22] Stone, M.H., *Healing the Mind: A History of Psychiatry from Antiquity to the Present*. London: Pimlico, 1998.

[23] Millon, T., *Masters of the Mind: Exploring the Story of Mental Illness from Ancient Times to the New Millennium*. Hoboken, New Jersey: John Wiley and Sons, Inc., 2004.

[24] Tuomy, M., *Treatise on the Principal Diseases of Dublin*. Dublin: William Folds, 1810.

[25] Weber, M.M., Emrich, H.M., 'Current and historical concepts of opiate treatment in psychiatric disorders'. *International Journal of Clinical Psychopharmacology* 1988; 3: 255-66; Leonard, E.C. Jr., 'Did some 18th and 19th century treatments for mental disorders act on the brain?' *Medical*

*Hypotheses* 2004; 62: 219-21; Breckenridge, A., 'William Withering's legacy – for the good of the patient'. *Clinical Medicine* 2006; 6: 393-7.

[26] Guthrie, D.A., *History of Medicine*. London: Thomas Nelson and Sons Limited, 1945; Fleetwood, J.F., *The History of Medicine in Ireland* (Second Edition). Dublin: Skellig Press, 1983; Farmar, *Patients, Potions and Physicians*.

[27] Merrit, H.H., Adams, R., Solomon, H.C., *Neurosyphilis*. Oxford: Oxford University Press, 1946; Brown, E.M., 'Why Wagner-Jauregg won the Nobel Prize for discovering malaria therapy for general paralysis of the insane'. *History of Psychiatry* 2000; 11: 371-82.

[28] Eager, R., 'A record of admissions to the mental section of the Lord Derby War Hospital, Warrington, from June 17th, 1916 to June 16th, 1917'. *Journal of Mental Science* 1918; 64: 272-96; pp. 286-7.

[29] Waugh, M.A., 'Alfred Fournier, 1832-1914: His influence on venereology'. *British Journal of Venereal Disease* 1974; 50: 232-6; Kelly, B.D., 'Dr William Saunders Hallaran and psychiatric practice in nineteenth-century Ireland'. *Irish Journal of Medical Science* 2008; 177: 79-84.

[30] Stone, *Healing the Mind*.

[31] Robins, *Fools and Mad*; Williamson, A.P., 'Psychiatry, moral management and the origins of social policy for mentally ill people in Ireland'. *Irish Journal of Medical Science* 1992; 161: 556-8; Shorter, E., *A History of Psychiatry: From the Era of the Asylum to the Age of Prozac*. New York: John Wiley and Sons, 1997; Kelly, B.D., 'Integrating psychological treatment approaches'. *Science* 2014; 344; 254-5.

[32] Psychiatrist. 'Insanity in Ireland'. *The Bell* 1944; 7: 303-10; Robins, *Fools and Mad*.

[33] Anonymous. Irish Division. *Journal of Mental Science* 1917; 63: 297-9; Reynolds, *Grangegorman*; pp. 218-9.

[34] Hallaran, *An Enquiry*; p. 1.

[35] Kelly, B.D., 'Dr William Saunders Hallaran and psychiatric practice in nineteenth-century Ireland'. *Irish Journal of Medical Science* 2008; 177: 79-84.

[36] Hallaran, *An Enquiry*; Hallaran, W.S., *Practical Observations on the Causes and Cures of Insanity* (Second Edition). Cork: Edwards and Savage, 1818; Fleetwood, J.F., *The History of Medicine in Ireland* (Second

Edition). Dublin: Skellig Press, 1983; Wade, N.J., 'The original spin doctors – the meeting of perception and insanity'. *Perception* 2005; 34: 253–60; Wade, N.J., Norrsell, U., Presly, A., 'Cox's chair 'a moral and a medical mean in the treatment of maniacs'. *History of Psychiatry* 2005; 16: 73–88.

[37] Cox, J.M., *Practical Observations on Insanity*. London: Baldwin and Murray, 1804; Cox, J.M., *Practical Observations on Insanity* (Second Edition). London: Baldwin and Murray, 1806.

[38] Cox, *Practical Observations on Insanity*; Stone, *Healing the Mind*; Porter, R., *Madmen: A Social History of Madhouses, Mad-Doctors and Lunatics*. Gloucestershire, United Kingdom: Tempus, 2004.

[39] Wade, N.J., 'The original spin doctors –the meeting of perception and insanity'. *Perception* 2005; 34: 253–60.

[40] Torrey, E., Miller, J., *The Invisible Plague: The Rise of Mental Illness from 1750 to the Present*. Piscataway, New Jersey: Rutgers University Press, 2001; Wade, N.J., Norrsell, U., Presly, A., 'Cox's chair 'a moral and a medical mean in the treatment of maniacs'. *History of Psychiatry* 2005; 16: 73–88.

[41] Hallaran, *An Enquiry*; pp. 63-4.

[42] United Nations. *Principles for the Protection of Persons with Mental Illness and the Improvement of Mental Health Care*. New York: United Nations, Secretariat Centre for Human Rights, 1991.

[43] Hallaran, *An Enquiry*.

[44] Hallaran, *Practical Observations on the Causes and Cures of Insanity*.

[45] Hallaran, *An Enquiry*; p. 10.

[46] Kelly, B.D., 'Dr William Saunders Hallaran and psychiatric practice in nineteenth-century Ireland'. *Irish Journal of Medical Science* 2008; 177: 79-84.

[47] Anonymous. Irish Division. *Journal of Mental Science* 1917; 63: 297-9; Reynolds, Grangegorman; pp. 218-9.

[48] Inspector of Lunatics (Ireland). *The Forty-Second Report (With Appendices) of the Inspector of Lunatics (Ireland)*. Dublin: Thom and Co./Her Majesty's Stationery Office, 1893; Walsh, D. and Daly, A., *Mental Illness in Ireland 1750–2002: Reflections on the Rise and Fall of Institutional Care*. Dublin: Health Research Board, 2004.

[49] Esquirol, J-É., *Des Passions*. Paris: Didot Jeune, 1805; Carlson, E.T., Dain, N., 'The psychotherapy that was moral treatment'. *American Journal of Psychiatry* 1960; 117: 519-24.

[50] Reuber, M., 'The architecture of psychological management: The Irish asylums (1801-1922)'. *Psychological Medicine* 1996; 26: 1179–89; Reuber, M., 'Moral management and the "unseen eye": Public lunatic asylums in Ireland, 1800–1845'. In: Malcolm, E., Jones, G. (eds) *Medicine, Disease and the State in Ireland, 1650-1940* (pp. 208–33). Cork: Cork University Press, 1999.

[51] Reynolds, J., *Grangegorman: Psychiatric Care in Dublin since 1815*. Dublin: Institute of Public Administration in association with Eastern Health Board, 1992.

[52] Hallaran, *An Enquiry*.

[53] Smith, L.. *'Cure, Comfort and Safe Custody': Public Lunatic Asylums in Early Nineteenth-Century England*. London and New York: Leicester University Press, 1999; p. 5.

[54] Esquirol, J-É., *Des Passions*. Paris: Didot Jeune, 1805.

[55] Carlson, E.T., Dain, N., 'The psychotherapy that was moral treatment'. *American Journal of Psychiatry* 1960; 117: 519-24.

[56] Inspector of Lunatic Asylums. *Report of the District, Local and Private Lunatic Asylums in Ireland 1846*. Dublin: Alexander Thom, for Her Majesty's Stationery Office, 1847; p. 19.

[57] Inspector of Lunatic Asylums, *Report of the District, Local and Private Lunatic Asylums in Ireland 1846*; p. 51.

[58] *Census of Ireland for the Year 1851 (Part III)*. Dublin: Thom and Sons, for Her Majesty's Stationery Office, 1854; p. 61.

[59] Lalor, J., 'On the use of education and training in the treatment of the insane in public lunatic asylums'. *Journal of the Statistical and Social Inquiry of Ireland* 1878; 7: 361–73; p. 362.

[60] Reynolds, *Grangegorman*.

[61] Tuke, D.H., 'On the Richmond Asylum schools'. *Journal of Mental Science* 1875; 21: 467-74; pp. 467-8.

[62] Anonymous. 'Obituary: Joseph Lalor, MD'. *Journal of Mental Science* 1886; 32: 462-3; p. 462.

[63] *Irish Times*, 5 August 1886.

[64] Inspector of Lunatics (Ireland). *The Forty-Second Report (With Appendices) of the Inspector of Lunatics (Ireland)*. Dublin: Thom and Co./ Her Majesty's Stationery Office, 1893; p. 9.

[65] Ibid, p. 6.

[66] Kelly, B.D., 'One hundred years ago: The Richmond Asylum, Dublin in 1907'. *Irish Journal of Psychological Medicine* 2007; 24: 108–14.

[67] Kelly, B.D. 'Criminal insanity in 19th-century Ireland, Europe and the United States: Cases, contexts and controversies'. *International Journal of Law and Psychiatry* 2009; 32: 362-8.

[68] McCandless, P., 'Curative asylum, custodial hospital: The South Carolina Lunatic Asylum and State Hospital, 1828–1920'. In: Porter, R., Wright, D. (eds.) *The Confinement of the Insane: International Perspectives, 1800– 1965* (pp. 173–92). Cambridge: Cambridge University Press, 2003.

[69] Wright, D., Moran, J.E., Gouglas, S., 'The confinement of the insane in Victorian Canada: The Hamilton and Toronto asylums, c. 1861–1891'. In: Porter, R., Wright, D. (eds) *The Confinement of the Insane: International Perspectives, 1800–1965* (pp. 100–28). Cambridge: Cambridge University Press, 2003.

[70] Inspector of Lunatics (Ireland), *The Forty-Second Report (With Appendices) of the Inspector of Lunatics (Ireland)*; p. 4.

[71] Ibid, p. 7.

[72] Ibid, pp. 145-6.

[73] Ibid, p. 146.

[74] Collins, A., 'Eleonora Fleury captured'. *British Journal of Psychiatry* 2013; 203: 5.

[75] Ibid.

# 2

# Establishing the Richmond War Hospital (1916)

> This Asylum [the Richmond District Asylum] was found in its customary good order.... A small separate block was placed by the Committee of Management at the disposal of the War Office for the use of mentally affected soldiers and has been freely availed of. – Inspectors of Lunatics (Ireland) (1916)[1]

The First World War commenced in mid-1914 when Austrian Archduke Franz Ferdinand was assassinated in the Bosnian capital, Sarajevo. The war lasted until 11 November 1918, when an armistice with Germany was signed in a railroad carriage at Compiègne, France. The war saw the Allied Powers, including the United Kingdom of Great Britain and Ireland, defeat the Central Powers, including most notably Germany. The total number of casualties in the war was 37 million, including over 16 million deaths, of which 10 million were military personnel. The First World War was remarkable not only for the number of deaths it caused, but also the technological sophistication of the conflict, which exposed soldiers and civilians to injury and killing on an unprecedented scale.

Over the course of the war, almost nine million soldiers served in the British army, of whom almost one million were killed. Over 200,000 Irish soldiers fought in the war, and an estimated 40,000 died in it.[2] Of these, up to 30,000 died while serving with the British army. Many more received physical injuries while in the British army or, as became apparent in the early years of the war, had to return home owing to mental troubles which occurred during the conflict and which, for many, seemed to be attributable to it.

At the same time as the First World War was taking place, Ireland was undergoing a period of intense political tumult as the Irish sought to break free of the United Kingdom of Great Britain and Ireland, of which it had been part since 1 January 1801. The struggle for Irish freedom had taken a new turn some decades earlier, in the late 1870s, as the Irish National Land League was founded in Castlebar, County Mayo on 21 October 1879. The Land League sought to support tenant farmers (predominantly Roman Catholic) in their conflicts with landlords (predominantly Protestant) regarding rent and land ownership. The organisation focussed on achieving the 'three Fs' for tenants: fair rent, fixity of tenure and free sale. Its first president was Charles Stuart Parnell (1846–91), an Irish landlord and later founder of the Irish Parliamentary Party (1882).

The establishment of the Land League was followed by a 'Land War' (1880-92) during which the Land League was declared illegal (1881). With many of the men of the Land League in prison, the Ladies Land League was founded in 1880 by Fanny Parnell (1848–82) and Anna Parnell (1852–1911), sisters of Charles Stuart Parnell. The Ladies Land League aimed to continue the work of the men in prison, and by 1882 had 500 branches throughout Ireland.

In parallel with the Land War, this period in Irish history also saw significant political developments in relation to self-government or 'home rule' for Ireland. In 1886, the Irish Government Bill was introduced, aiming to establish home rule in Ireland, but was defeated by thirty votes in the House of Commons. Seven years later, a second Home Rule Bill was defeated in the House of Lords and it was not until 1914 that another Home Rule Bill (the Government of Ireland Act 1914) was finally passed, although this never came into force owing, in large part, to the occurrence of the First World War (1914-18).

Against this background, there was inevitable political unrest in Ireland during the First World War and this culminated in the Easter Rising in April 1916, which had a significant effect on practices at the Richmond Asylum in Dublin, just two months before the arrival of the Richmond War Hospital there in June 1916.

## The Easter Rising and the Diagnosis of 'Shock' at the Richmond District Asylum

The Easter Rising began on 24 April 1916 and lasted for six days. In essence, Irish nationalist rebels sought to establish an Irish Republic, independent of Great Britain. The Rising was largely organised by the Irish Republican Brotherhood which had been founded in the 1850s with the aim of achieving an independent democratic republic in Ireland. To this end, members of nationalist organisations including the Irish Volunteers, Irish Citizens Army and Cumann na mBan (Women's Legue) seized control of key locations in Dublin over Easter 1916. An Irish republic was declared and a provisional government established at the General Post Office on Sackville Street (later O'Connell Street) in Dublin's city centre, not very far from the Richmond Asylum.

The Rising which had been scheduled for Easter Sunday did not commence until Easter Monday, leading to considerable confusion. Some potential participants, including members of Cumann na mBan, had expected manoeuvres rather than an uprising on Easter Sunday.[3] When military activity finally commenced on Easter Monday, public confusion about unfolding events meant there was an insufficient groundswell of support for the rebels among the general Irish population. The rebels were, in any case, no military match for the British forces, and the Rising was crushed relatively quickly. Padraig Pearse (1879–1916) and fourteen other leaders, including Pearse's brother Willie (1881–1916), were court-martialled and executed by firing squad. Roger Casement (1864–1916), an Irish nationalist and poet, was hanged at Pentonville Prison in England.

One of the leaders executed for his part in the Rising was Thomas McDonagh (1878–1916), an Irish nationalist, poet, playwright and educationalist. Following his execution, McDonagh's body was buried in a pit and covered with quicklime in Arbour Hill in Dublin. McDonagh was soon immortalised in a poem by Francis Ledwidge (1887–1917), titled 'Thomas McDonagh'.[4]

Ledwidge was an Irish war poet from Slane, County Meath. A nationalist and patriot, Ledwidge co-founded a branch of the Irish Volunteers before volunteering for the army and serving in the Dardanelles and elsewhere. In 1916, Ledwidge, like many other nationalist soldiers, had a complex response to news of the Easter Rising[5] and his lament for Thomas McDonagh echoes both his sadness at the loss of McDonagh and his more general despair at the plight of the nationalist cause in Ireland. The following year, Ledwidge was tragically killed in action at the Battle of Passchendaele (at which Gunner KL had also served; see Introduction).

Notwithstanding the lack of co-ordination, general confusion and significant disappointment surrounding the Easter Rising, military activity was not confined to Dublin. In Ashbourne, County Meath, there was a substantial attack on a Royal Irish Constabulary Barracks. In Cork, 1,200 volunteers assembled, under the command of Tomás Mac Curtain (1884–1920), although they did not engage in action owing to confusion about their orders. In Wexford, one hundred volunteers took over the town of Enniscorthy for three days, before British reinforcements were dispatched; rebel leaders were escorted to Arbour Hill Prison in Dublin and ordered by Pearse to surrender. There was also significant military action in Country Galway, where Dr Ada English (1875–1944), an asylum-doctor in Ballinasloe, was active in the Irish Volunteers and Cumann na mBan.[6] Military activity in Galway was led by Liam Mellows (1895–1922), an Irish nationalist and Sinn Féin politician.[7]

In Dublin, the Rising predated the establishment of the Richmond War Hospital by two months but had an interesting effect on admission patterns to the main Richmond Asylum. Collins, in his seminal work on effects of the Rising on the Richmond, notes, in the first instance, the generally disturbing effect that the Rising likely had on residents of central Dublin, where the Richmond was located:

> 1916 Dublin had a large Protestant and unionist population augmented by a relatively loyal Catholic bourgeoisie and an urban working class often dependent on the receipts from their menfolk in the service of the crown. There was an initial horror by many of these elements at the outbreak of violence and the destruction of parts of the city.[8]

In terms of medical care for the wounded, a Red Cross Hospital with 250 beds had already been established in Dublin Castle to care for soldiers wounded in France, and the King George

V military hospital (now St. Bricin's Hospital) provided a further 462 beds. Despite these measures, however, various other Dublin hospitals, including the psychiatric institutions, were soon to become involved in the 1916 conflict, both in terms of providing care to those affected and simply getting caught in the cross-fire.

At St Patrick's Hospital, for example, the RMS Dr Richard Leper reported to the Board of Governors that 'we have been in the centre of a battlefield for 10 days surrounded by the armies and this experience is one that few have experienced':

> On my arrival here from Lucan on Easter Monday firing commenced all round this district and continued more or less constantly for 10 days. At many times the rattle of machine gun fire was often continuous for hours and the bullets came into the wards in several places... Bullets entered the New Wing and raked the top ward on the ladies side. When this began I personally placed barricades and padding material such as mattresses in the windows. It seems most wonderful that none of the patients or nurses were killed as the fire lasted for several hours. A guard of 40 soldiers were at the Front gate and I and my wife fed these men as well as we could during the rebellion. My greatest anxiety at first was that the Hospital would be occupied by the Rebels....[9]

Across the river Liffey, at the Richmond, the RMS Dr John O'Conor Donelan described Easter week as 'a rather anxious period' and reported 'belligerents' firing into the asylum grounds:

> A rebellion has come and gone, and now that we are able to review the situation it is gratifying to find that our institution has not suffered by the incident.... It is a matter of satisfaction at being able to state that neither amongst the patients or staff was there a single casualty, nor did the buildings suffer in any way, although the belligerents

on both sides were constantly firing through the grounds. Immediately we found we were in the danger zone we removed the patients from exposed positions; at night their mattresses were placed on the floor, and, of course, they were confined to the house during the disturbance. The gate lodge at Burnswick Street and the grounds in the neighbourhood were occupied by the insurgents for a day and a half, but further than constructing a barricade they did no damage.[10]

The Rising ended on 29 April as the rebels suffered a definitive military defeat, and many of its leaders were executed. While admission rates at the Richmond fell during the Rising itself, the following weeks produced an interesting change in admission patterns: on 1 May, a woman was admitted with a diagnosis of 'melancholia due to shock' which, as Collins points out, 'may be the first occasion that the word 'shock' appears in the admission books of Grangegorman'.[11] The diagnosis of 'shock' was to appear some ten times at the Richmond during the month of May, immediately following the Rising:

> As the diagnosis of 'shock' does not appear to occur in the admission books prior to May 24 1916, it is reasonable to consider its presence for diagnostic purposes as indicative of an admission where the rebellion was deemed to be central to the presentation.... There were 10 'shock' admissions in all, that is, admissions that the admitting doctor believed were due to the rebellion.... Of the 10 individuals admitted with 'shock', nine were females. After May 31 the diagnosis does not recur and admission rates in general normalise... The individuals are mostly female but they also tended to reside in those parts of the city most affected by the trouble. Their presentations vary from 'melancholia due to shock' to 'mania secondary to shock' to 'confusional insanity due to shock'.[12]

At St Patrick's Hospital, too, Leper reported to the Governors that two admissions during 'the height of the rebellion' were 'produced by shock and terror caused by the insurrection'; in one case, the army ambulance 'was fired on whilst conveying the patient to the Hospital'.[13] Leper's phraseology, especially his use of the word 'terror', has echoes of the wording used by Hallaran in Cork more than a century earlier, when, in his 1810 textbook, Hallaran speculated on the possible 'cause of the extraordinary increase of insanity in Ireland' and concluded that the 'terror' of the Irish Rebellion of 1798 and its aftermath played significant roles in the apparent increase in insanity in Cork:

> To account therefore correctly for this unlooked for pressure of a public and private calamity, it appears to be indispensably requisite to take into account the high degree of corporeal as well as of mental excitement, which may be supposed a consequence of continued warfare in the general sense.... In some it was evident that terror merely had its sole influence, producing in most instances an incurable melancholia. In others where disappointed ambition had been prevalent, the patients were of an opposite cast, and were in general cheerful, gay and fanciful; but extremely treacherous and vindictive.[14]

Over a hundred years later, the relationship between the diagnosis 'shock', as used at the Richmond in May 1916 (as well as the 'shock and terror' described at St Patrick's Hospital) and the later diagnosis 'shell shock', as it relates to soldiers in the First World War at the Richmond War Hospital, is not clear. Indeed, as Collins notes, 'at this distance, it is difficult to establish whether the diagnosis of 'shock' as it relates to these patients has any relationship to the concept of 'shell-shock' that had been described in British soldiers on the western Front'.[15] Notwithstanding these uncertainties, however, it is clear that the Easter Rising produced a significant change in admission patterns at the Richmond Asylum in Dublin, and that the word 'shock' came into prominent diagnostic use in the month following the Rising, which was also the month prior to the opening of the War Hospital, on 16 June 1916.

## Establishing the Richmond War Hospital

In January 1916, Donelan, RMS of the Richmond, reported to the Richmond District Asylum Committee that the British military authorities sought accommodation to use as an 'observation hospital' for soldiers with nervous and mental troubles.[16] The need for such a facility had become apparent over the previous two years as the First World War progressed. While the physical injuries sustained by soldiers were increasingly expected and managed throughout a network of hospitals and clinics devoted to the care of the physically wounded, there was much greater confusion and uncertainty regarding soldiers with mental problems which manifested during the war and appeared, in at least some cases, to be attributable to experiences in battle.

The most puzzling aspect of this emergent problem was the lack of any consistent association between identifiable physical injuries and the psychological symptoms with which soldiers presented, including loss of memory, dizziness, tremor, headache, poor concentration, tinnitus and hypersensitivity to noise.[17] The term 'shell shock' evolved to describe such cases which developed following exposure to shell fire but were not associated with identifiable physical injury.

These cases presented a real challenge to the British army because medical officers who usually identified physically wounded soldiers requiring treatment back home, were increasingly coming across psychological or psychiatric cases and did not know how to proceed. As a result, a series of psychiatric facilities throughout Great Britain and Ireland was made available to assess and treat such soldiers when they were sent back from the Front. Many of the war hospitals, dealing with physical and/or psychiatric problems, were located in pre-existing psychiatric hospitals, which were adapted especially for the purpose.

The process of conversion of psychiatric hospitals to war hospitals was often a complex one, involving extensive changes to physical infrastructure (for example, installing x-ray machines) as well as intricate staffing rearrangements.[18] Nonetheless, by 1919 there were, in England and Wales, 24 mental hospitals being used as war hospitals, 14 of which were for physically sick and wounded soldiers only; seven of which were for nervous problems only; and three of which were for both physical and mental problems.[19]

In Ireland, the Richmond War Hospital, located on the grounds of the Richmond District Asylum, Grangegorman, opened its doors on 16 June 1916. While the War Hospital was an administrative element within the larger institution, the War Hospital was, in many important respects, separate from the main asylum. In the first instance, a new and separate block was put at the disposal of the army for the War Hospital, and its patients did not appear on the main asylum's record books.[20] Moreover, the army agreed to pay 21 shillings a week per occupied bed – a rate that was distinctly advantageous for the asylum managers: the weekly cost per patient was under 14 shillings and the army provided clothing for its own patients, making the arrangement an especially lucrative one from the asylum's perspective.[21] The War Hospital was to cater for 32 soldiers at a time.

As Reynolds notes in his history of Grangegorman, the War Hospital was staffed by Richmond Asylum staff, but this arrangement was not without complexity:

The head night attendant, William Culverwell, objected to doing duty in the [war] hospital. 'He is the only employee lay or medical', Donelan [RMS] told the joint committee, 'who has hesitated to assist in relieving the sufferings of those brave soldiers who have risked their lives and sacrificed their health in their country's service.' He added that Culverwell's duty was simply supervision, and since he considered the attendant supervised was more reliable than the head night attendant, he recommended that Culverwell should not be permitted access to the war hospital in the future. The committee members contented themselves with ordering that Culverwell perform the duties placed on him by the medical superintendent.[22]

The reasons for Culverwell's objections to the War Hospital are not recorded and may have been attributable to internal asylum politics rather than any particular objection to 'relieving the sufferings of those brave soldiers who have risked their lives and sacrificed their health in their country's service.' What is clear, however, is that following its opening in 1916, soldiers began to arrive at the Richmond War Hospital with all of the signs and symptoms of shell shock and various other mental and physical disorders that were increasingly described in the medical literature of the time.[23] The *Richmond War Hospital Case Book* provides excellent clinical descriptions of such cases, of which the case of Captain BC is a good example.[24]

Captain BC, a 23-year old Roman Catholic captain in the British army, was admitted to the Richmond War Hospital owing to the 'hardships of war' and 'being buried by shell fire'. The admitting officer noted that Captain BC 'seems rather weak and emotional. Tongue tremulous [i.e. shaky].... Fine tremor of limbs'. From a psychological point of view, Captain BC was 'dull, depressed and confused ... replies more by motion of his head; in this way he indicates he has pain and noises in his head and that he hears voices and that something is following him. He, after some time, told me verbally, on my questioning him more closely, that he was blown up by a shell behind the lines. He seems rather nervous and apprehensive'.

Six days after admission to the War Hospital, there was 'much improvement. He is brighter and more communicative and seems less nervous, He sleeps fairly well'. One week later, Captain BC continued 'to improve. He is bright and cheerful in his manner, but still complains of feeling nervous. The headache is much less and he is not now troubled by voices'. One month after admission, Captain BC was 'bright and cheerful and states he is now feeling all right He states he has not felt as well for a long time'. One month later again, Captain BC was 'perfectly rational' and was sleeping and eating well. Within two weeks, he was discharged.

Based on these records, it is apparent that Captain BC displayed many symptoms typical of soldiers with mental troubles in the context of the First World War: apprehension, nervousness, trembling limbs, low mood and initial difficulty speaking of his experiences in battle. Relatively quickly, however, his headache resolved and he appeared 'bright and cheerful'. Soon, Captain BC was ready to leave the War Hospital.

The treatment of soldiers like Captain BC was an important task from both medical and military perspectives, and this was one of the key reasons why the Richmond War Hospital was closely monitored by the War Office throughout its existence. Indeed, while the Richmond District Asylum committee managed the War Hospital on a day-to-day basis, at no point did the War Office relinquish control of the soldiers admitted to it. A letter from the Lieutenant Colonel at the King George V Hospital, Dublin, addressed to the RMS of the Richmond, dated 1 August 1916, was emphatic on this point:

Please note that all Soldier Patients transferred to Richmond Asylum War Hospital remain under the control of the War Office, and as Officer in Charge of King George Vth Hospital (Central Hospital) I am responsible for them no matter in what part of your Asylum they may have to be accommodated, until such time as they are invalided from the Army.[25]

Captain BC's recovery from his symptoms was by no means unique, as very many soldiers were discharged from the War Hospital having apparently recovered from their symptoms.[26] Driver AB is another good example of this, with a symptom profile and outcome that are similar but not quite identical to those of Captain BC.

Driver AB was a 30-year-old, Roman Catholic army driver who was admitted to the Richmond War Hospital having apparently 'deserted while stationed' in a barracks in Southern Ireland. Clinical notes record that on admission Driver AB's 'tongue [was] tremulous. Fine tremor of limbs. Scars on left forearm'. Mentally, Driver AB was 'very dull and confused and has delusions of persecution arising out of hallucinations of sight and hearing':

> He is so confused he does not realise where he is and speaks at time as if he believed he was in France. He states a whole crowd of them were following him with knives all day and that they did the same last night and followed him up the lines with the ammunition. When questioned more closely he asked: 'The guns are coming out of aren't they? Aren't they coming up for a rest?' He states he hears everyone talking about him but cannot tell what they say. When questioned if he were in France said 'Yes' and then 'No. I remember now. I'm in Ireland, aren't I? I think I am'.

Six days after admission, Driver AB was 'much improved. He states he does not now hear the voices. The memory is much clearer. He is, however, dull at times. He complains of some loss of power in his arm.... He is very quiet and gives no trouble. Eats and sleeps well.' One week later, Driver AB was 'very much improved. He is, however, rather giddy and silly in his manner and is undoubtedly somewhat weak-minded. He is, however, well-conducted' and 'sleeps and eats well.'

One month after admission, Driver AB was 'bright and cheerful. Gives no trouble. He states his head is now all right.' Two months after admission he was 'now rational ... bright and cheerful.' A few weeks later, Driver AB was 'discharged, recovered.'

Both Captain BC and Driver AB had apparently good outcomes from their time in the Richmond War Hospital as both were discharged having apparently recovered from their symptoms. In addition, both had many symptoms in common, including trembling limbs, low mood and confusion. Both, however, also had some worrying severe psychiatric symptoms including hearing voices or other noises, and the paranoid belief that they were being followed. Clearly, these were cases of serious psychological or psychiatric disturbance, however short-lived, and the Richmond War Hospital, like all the war hospitals, was clearly moving into diagnostic and therapeutic territories that were as challenging as they were uncharted. The diagnostic challenges they faced, and the symptoms soldiers described, are considered in some detail in the next chapter.

### Endnotes

[1] Inspectors of Lunatics (Ireland). *The Sixty-Sixth Annual Report (With Appendices) of the Inspectors of Lunatics (Ireland), Being for the Year Ending 31st December 1916.* Dublin: His Majesty's Stationery Office, 1918; pp. xxi-xxii.

[2] The precise figure is not known; see: Ferriter, D., *The Transformation of Ireland, 1900-2000.* London: Profile Books, 2004; p. 132; McGreevy, R.,

'Number of Irish in both wars unknown'. *Irish Times* 2014; June 9; Myers, K., 'Crunching the numbers and busting myths'. *History Ireland* 2014; 22: 40-1.

[3] McCarthy, C., *Cumann na mBan and the Irish Revolution*. Dublin: The Collins Press, 2007; p. 53.

[4] Ledwidge, F., *Francis Ledwidge: Complete Poems* (edited by Alice Curtayne). London: Martin Brian & O'Keefe, 1974; p. 153. For further Irish war poetry, see: Dawe, G. (ed.). *Earth Voices Whispering: An Anthology of Irish War Poetry, 1914-1945*. Belfast: Blackstaff Press, 2008. See also, in relation to Craiglockhart War Hospital, Edinburgh: Stewart, A., 'Wilfred Owen: Hospital poet'. *British Journal of Psychiatry* 2013; 203: 195.

[5] See also Barry, S., *A Long Long Way*. London, Faber and Faber Limited, 2005.

[6] Davoren, M., Breen, E.G., Kelly, B.D., 'Dr Adeline English: Revolutionizing politics and psychiatry in Ireland'. *Irish Psychiatrist* 2009; 10: 260-2; Kelly, B., Davoren, M., 'Dr Ada English'. In: Mulvihill, M. (ed), *Lab Coats and Lace: The Lives and Legacies of Inspiring Irish Women Scientists and Pioneers* (p. 97). Dublin: Women in Technology and Science, 2009; Davoren, M., Breen, E.G., Kelly, B.D., 'Dr Ada English: Patriot and psychiatrist in early 20th century Ireland'. *Irish Journal of Psychological Medicine* 2011; 28: 91-6; Kelly, B.D., 'Dr Ada English (1875–1944): Doctor, patriot, politician'. *British Journal of Psychiatry* 2014; 204: 5; Kelly, B.D., *Ada English: Patriot and Psychiatrist*. Sallins, Co Kildare: Irish Academic Press, 2014.

[7] Greaves, C.D., *Liam Mellows and the Irish Revolution*. Belfast: An Ghlór Gafa, 2004.

[8] Collins, A., 'The Richmond District Asylum and the 1916 Easter Rising', *Irish Journal of Psychological Medicine* 2013; 30: 279-83; p. 279.

[9] 'Dr Richard Leper's report to the Governors of St Patrick's Hospital, 3 June 1916'. Quoted in: *Malcolm E. Swift's Hospital: A History of St Patrick's Hospital, Dublin, 1746-1989*. Dublin: Gill and Macmillan, 1989; pp. 326-7.

[10] Donelan, J. O'Conor. *Report to the Governors of the Richmond District Asylum*, 1916, 11 May.

[11] Collins, A., 'The Richmond District Asylum and the 1916 Easter Rising'. *Irish Journal of Psychological Medicine* 2013; 30: 279-83; p. 280.

[12] Ibid, p. 281.

[13] Dr Richard Leper's report to the Governors of St Patrick's Hospital, 3 June 1916. Quoted in: Malcolm, *Swift's Hospital*; p. 326.

[14] Hallaran, W.S., *An Enquiry into the Causes Producing the Extraordinary Addition to the Number of Insane together with Extended Observations on the Cure of Insanity with Hints as to the Better Management of Public Asylums for Insane Persons.* Cork: Edwards and Savage, 1810; pp. 12-3.

[15] Collins, A., 'The Richmond District Asylum and the 1916 Easter Rising'. *Irish Journal of Psychological Medicine* 2013; 30: 279-83; p. 281. See also: Myers, C.S., 'A contribution to the study of shell shock'. *Lancet* 1915; 185: 316-20.

[16] Reynolds, J., *Grangegorman: Psychiatric Care in Dublin since 1815.* Dublin: Institute of Public Administration in association with Eastern Health Board, 1992; p. 217.

[17] Jones, E., Fear, N.T., Wessely, S., 'Shell shock and mild traumatic brain injury: A historical review'. *American Journal of Psychiatry* 2007; 164: 1641-5; pp. 1641-2.

[18] Thomson, D.G., 'A descriptive record of the conversion of a county asylum into a war hospital for sick and wounded soldiers in 1915'. *Journal of Mental Science* 1916; 62: 109-35; Vincent, W., 'Use of asylums as military hospitals'. *Journal of Mental Science* 1916; 62: 174-8; Hotchkis, R.D., 'Renfrew District Asylum as a war hospital for mental invalids: Some contrasts in administration with an analysis of cases admitted during the first year'. *Journal of Mental Science* 1917; 63: 238-49.

[19] Anonymous. Review of: The Sixth Annual Report of the Board of Control for the year 1919; history of the asylum war hospitals in England and Wales: Report to the Secretary of State for the Home Department by Sir Marriott Cooke, K.B.E., M.B., and C. Hubert Bond, C.B.E., M.D., D.Sc., F.R.C.P., Commissioners of the Board of Control. *Journal of Mental Science* 1921; 67: 484-92.

[20] Collins, A., 'The Richmond District Asylum and the 1916 Easter Rising'. *Irish Journal of Psychological Medicine* 2013; 30: 279-83.

[21] Reynolds, *Grangegorman*; p. 217.

[22] Ibid, pp. 217-8.

[23] Myers, C.S., 'A contribution to the study of shell shock'. *Lancet* 1915; 185: 316-20.

[24] *Richmond War Hospital Case Book (1918-1919)*, National Archives of Ireland, Bishop Street, Dublin 8 (BR/PRIV 1223 Richmond War).

[25] *Richmond War Hospital Admission and Discharge Book for Field Service (1916-1919)*, National Archives of Ireland, Bishop Street, Dublin 8 (BR/ PRIV 1223 Richmond War).

[26] Quoted in: Reynolds, *Grangegorman*; p. 219.

# 3

# 'He Lost Himself Completely': War Trauma at the Richmond War Hospital

The diagnosis of 'shell shock' was both common and controversial during the First World War and its immediate aftermath.[1] Prior to this period, common diagnoses in Irish asylums included mania, melancholia, mono-mania and dementia, some of which correspond, at least in part, to contemporary diagnoses of bipolar affective disorder, depression and schizophrenia.[2] Interpreting diagnoses from the past is, however, a complex exercise. Not only do diagnostic practices change over time, but official clinical records can be shaped by the individuals writing them to reflect certain versions of events; for example, the clinical record can be used to show that the doctor behaved in a fashion that was entirely appropriate, logical and sympathetic, even if that was not always the case.[3] As a result, interpreting clinical records from the past requires both thought and caution.

Nonetheless, compared to historical analyses which focus primarily on the histories of psychiatric institutions or mental health legislation, approaches based on clinical records move at least somewhat towards historian Roy Porter's idea of 'medical history from below' (that is, from the level of the patient experience),[4] even though they still rely on records written by medical superintendents and others, rather than direct patient accounts, such as patients' letters.[5]

The central merit of approaches based on clinical records, however, is that such records are uniquely useful for identifying shifts in clinical practice over time and conveying the complexity of hospital life.[6] Moreover, since clinical records reflect both the patients' behaviour *and* the interpretation of such behaviour by medical authorities, diagnoses in clinical records reflect unique and crucial accounts of patients' experiences – accounts which generally played important roles in determining how patients were treated in and by institutions.

In this context, it is interesting that the advent of the First World War was to change the diagnostic profile of patient populations in certain asylums throughout the United Kingdom of Great Britain and Ireland,[7] including the Richmond Asylum, as soldiers returning from the Front were admitted in increasing numbers. Against this background, this chapter examines the emergence of the diagnosis of 'shell shock' during the First World War and explores key symptoms described in soldiers admitted to the Richmond War Hospital between 1916 and 1919.

## The Diagnosis of Shell Shock

During the First World War, cases of the syndrome which would become known as 'shell shock' began to present in 1914 and the condition quickly became a substantial problem for all armies; in some areas, nervous disorders accounted for 40% of all casualties.[8] There was already a significant pre-history to the idea of shell shock,[9] as nervous and mental symptoms following warfare were described in literature as far back as Homer's *Iliad* and the diaries of Samuel Pepys (1633–1703).[10] In addition, the late 1800s saw the emergence of a condition known as 'railway spine', described by John Eric Erichsen and characterised by post-traumatic symptoms in passengers involved in railroad accidents, which were relatively common.[11] Victims of 'railway spine' described symptoms in the absence of apparent physical injury and there was considerable controversy as to whether or not these cases stemmed from subtle damage to the brain and spine, or were attributable to 'hysteria' (conversion disorder); the same debate would later emerge regarding shell shock (see below).

All major wars in recent history have been associated with specific nervous syndromes including, for example, 'disordered action of the heart' (DAH), diagnosed following the South African War (1899–1902) and characterised by palpitation, breathlessness, chest pain and exhaustion.[12] This condition was also known as neuro-circulatory asthenia (in the United States), effort syndrome, and irritable heart of soldiers (Da Costa syndrome). Other terms included nostalgia neurasthenia and psychogenic rheumatism.[13]

These were relatively common syndromes, of great concern to military commanders. One study of 5,500 soldiers admitted to the medical division of the Royal Victoria Hospital in Netley, England after serving abroad between 1863 and 1866, showed that 8 per cent had been invalided out with apparent heart problems.[14] Similar reports from the United States confirmed that apparent DAH was a significant problem among troops there too, and was very difficult to explain in purely physical terms. Similarly, during the Boer War many soldiers diagnosed with rheumatism showed few signs of the disease following discharge, raising significant questions about the true origin of their symptoms during and immediately following the war.[15]

During the First World War, however, there was a veritable epidemic of shell shock between July and December 1916, when some 16,000 cases were recorded in the British army alone, during the Battle of the Somme. Overall, 10 per cent of British casualties in the war had some form of shell shock or neurasthenia (anxiety, fatigue, neuralgia, headache, depressed mood),[16] and shell shock accounted for one-seventh of all discharges from the British army.[17]

At a relatively early stage, two types of shell shock seemed to emerge: neurasthenic and hysterical.[18] Neurasthenic shell shock was thought to affect commissioned officers only, and presented with symptoms of severe anxiety, fatigue, neuralgia (pain), headache and low mood – a collection of symptoms not dissimilar to certain features in contemporary conceptualisations of post-traumatic stress disorder (PTSD).[19] The hysterical variety of shell shock was more likely to be diagnosed in enlisted soldiers, owing to their perceived lower educational attainment and social class, and was chiefly characterised by hysterical symptoms such as mutism or fugue (periods of memory loss).

The term 'shell shock' gained particular currency in medical circles following its use by Captain Charles S. Myers in the *Lancet* in February 1915.[20] The following year, again in the *Lancet*, Myers associated an especially broad variety of symptoms with shell shock, ranging from deficits of memory, vision, smell and taste, to over-reaction and 'hyperaesthesia' (increased sensitivity in one or more body areas).[21] As a result of this medical attention, and the clear problems it posed on the battlefield, the diagnosis of shell shock was in relatively widespread use by the time the Richmond War Hospital opened in 1916.[22] By June 1918, there were some 22 special hospitals throughout Great Britain and Ireland,[23] and shell shock was a key diagnosis.[24]

Despite increased recognition of the problems presented by shell shock, however, there was still considerable disagreement about its causes. Initially, shell shock was conceived as being the result of physical injury to the brain and thus a primarily neurological disorder.[25] Soon, however, theories emerged that rather than being a direct result of physical trauma, shellshock was fundamentally psychological in origin,[26] a result of 'intense and frequently-repeated emotion' owing to battlefield experiences, compounded by 'loss of sleep from external causes'.[27]

The association between shell shock and soldiers' direct experience of shell fire supported both physical and psychological theories of causation and did not assist greatly in distinguishing between the two. The case of Gunner GH, admitted to the Richmond War Hospital in late 1918, demonstrates many of the mental and physical features typical in cases of shell shock at the War Hospital.

Gunner GH was a 38-year-old Roman Catholic soldier, admitted to the War Hospital directly from King George V Hospital, a non-psychiatric hospital in Dublin. On admission to the War Hospital, Gunner GH's tongue and limbs were 'tremulous' and his 'front of head perspiring'. Mentally, he was 'dull and somewhat depressed and worried'. Gunner GH described 'pain and bursting noises in his head. He 'states when he drops off to sleep he wakes up in a fright and fancies someone is about his bed. In his dreams he imagines he is running'. These features were typical of shell shock: nervousness, tremor, pain, insomnia, bad dreams, low mood and hearing noises reminiscent of the battlefield.

The medical officer noted that Gunner GH also complained 'much of perspiration over front part of his head and states that whenever he comes before a Military Board he loses control over himself. I notice he slurs some of his words and finds it very difficult to pronounce test expressions. He is in much worry about his wife and child. The child is ill and his wife cannot speak well'.

Gunner GH had initially joined the army in 1900; he re-joined in 1914; went to the Front in 1916; and 'came home [in 1918] suffering from neurasthenia and was marked [that is, di-agnosed with] shell shock afterwards. Had venereal [disease] (gonorrhoea) in Gibraltar when a young fellow. States he was caught in the middle of a field under shell fire in October 1917 but kept on and then broke down completely last April and was sent home'.

The diagnoses of 'neurasthenia' and 'shell shock' in this case are consistent with the neurasthenic rather than hysterical va-riety of shell shock, although it is notable that Gunner GH's speech appears to have been affected also, impairing his perfor-mance at the 'Military Board' to review his case.

On his first night at the Richmond War Hospital, Gunner GH 'remained quiet and slept well'. After one week he was 'very much improved' and 'getting more control over himself. He is not nervous when questioned. He states his head is less trouble-some. Sleeps and eats well'. After a further week, Gunner GH was 'very much improved. He is allowed out on pass every day for a walk. He is brighter and more cheerful and is far less nervous. Sleeps and eats well'. Four weeks after admission this improvement was sustained: Gunner GH was 'much improved in his appearance; he is fairly rational in his conversation but is somewhat nervous on examination. He has been very well conducted since admission.... Sleeps and eats well'. Three weeks later, Gunner GH was discharged from the War Hospital.

The case of Gunner GH is typical of many at the Richmond War Hospital, with a clear history of exposure to shell fire, mul-tiple symptoms of shell shock, and a considerable degree of ap-parent recovery after just a few weeks in the War Hospital. The case of Private JK, also admitted in late 1918, is another good example, with an especially vivid account of exposure to shell fire and its traumatic consequences.

Private JK, was a 19-year-old, single private who, like Gunner GH, was admitted to the War Hospital from King George V Hospital, Dublin. Private JK had been in the army for a year and a half and, on admission to the Richmond War Hospital, was described as 'stout and strong'; with 'alopecia areata' [patchy hair loss, generally on the scalp]; 'tongue tremulous'; and with 'tremor of right hand'. Like Gunner GH, Private JK seemed 'slightly depressed' and 'complains of pain in his head and states he sleeps badly and is disturbed by dreams when he does sleep'.

Private JK had joined the army in 1917 and went to the Front in 1918. He was 'there for five months' but 'was blown up and buried for 36 hours' near Kemmel, a village six miles southwest of Ypres in Belgium, scene of intense, sustained battles. Private JK 'got shell shock' as a result of his experiences and spent time in various hospitals including the Hermitage Hospital in Lucan,[28] although he reportedly 'felt depressed at Lucan because it was lonely there'.

On his first night at the Richmond War Hospital, Private JK 'remained quiet and slept well'. One week after admission, he had 'improved considerably. He is fairly bright and cheerful. He complains of pain and dizziness in his head occasionally. Sleeps and eat well'. Two weeks after admission, Private JK was transferred to Belfast War Hospital for further treatment.

The trauma-related symptoms experienced by Private JK ('blown up and buried for 36 hours') were clearly attributable to exposure to shell fire in the battlefield. In other cases, however, it appears that an initial diagnosis of shell shock was compounded by further or repeated exposure to different injury or trauma, cumulatively resulting in admission to the Richmond War Hospital. Gunner MN, for example, was a 35-year-old, Roman Catholic gunner admitted to the Richmond War Hospital in 1919 with a diagnosis of 'shell shock'. On admission, Gunner MN was 'pale, thin and worn-looking. Tongue tremulous'. Mentally, he was 'dull and more-or-less apathetic. His memory is bad and he complains of insomnia. He states he used to suffer from headache after long spells of firing and occasional attacks of vertigo. He puts it that from what he hears he 'lost himself' completely for a time. He states he got an injury on his head from the march to Germany. He fell and cut his head and got unconscious for a time. He felt drowsy and stupor came over him. There is a tear on the forehead just at the root of the hair where he states he was injured'.

Gunner MN had joined the army in late 1914 'and went to the Front sometime in 1915. Came home suffering from shell shock in the summer 1916 and went back again. He is unable to give even approximate dates'. The day after his admission to the Richmond War Hospital, Gunner MN 'remained quiet and slept well during the night'. One week after admission, he was 'looking much better. He is not quite as pale as he was. He states he is feeling better. He is beginning to brighten up and his memory is improved. He sleeps well, Appetite good'.

One week later, after a fortnight in the War Hospital, Gunner MN was 'very much improved in every way. He is bright and cheerful. Joins in games and does a little ward work. He states he is feeling very well now. His memory is fair. Sleeps and eats well'. One month later, Gunner MN had been 'suffering from suppurating bunion for past week. It is now almost well. Mentally, he is much improved. He is bright and cheerful. Very well-conducted. He sleeps and eats well'.

Two months after admission, Gunner MN was 'very quiet and well-conducted as a rule. He expresses no delusions and his memory is improving. He states his head seldom troubles him now. Sleeps and eats well'. The following month, clinical notes record that Gunner MN 'seems fairly rational He is, however, of low cerebration [intelligence]. Sleeps and eats well'. This general improvement was sustained and, five months after admission, Gunner MN was discharged to the 'care of friend'. Clearly, the accumulated traumatic effects of the war had subsided, at least to a certain extent, during Gunner MN's time at the War Hospital.

## 'He States He Has Nothing To Live For': Melancholia at the War Hospital

Many of the cases admitted to the Richmond War Hospital were characterised not only by characteristic symptoms of neurasthenic or hysterical shell shock, but also features of depression, which was a relatively common feature of shell shock but could also attain considerable severity in its own right. Corporal IJ, for example, was a 26-year-old, single Wesleyan admitted to the Richmond War Hospital in late 1918. Corporal IJ was described as 'stout'; complained of a cough; and seemed mentally 'somewhat depressed, and hypochondriacal'. Corporal IJ complained 'of pain and 'clattering' noises in his head. He states his head jumps now and then, and that he sleeps badly and dreams much. He states he has nothing to live for'.

Corporal IJ had joined the army in 1914 and spent time in India, only to return in 1915 when 'he used to suffer with his head and ears'. He then returned to Ireland and had 'been in several hospital since he came home', suffering with 'influenza and pneumonia'. On his first night at the Richmond War Hospital, Corporal IJ 'remained quiet and slept well'. One week after admission, Corporal IJ remained 'dull and depressed and inclined to be hypochondriacal. He is very nervous. He took a peculiar cold shiver while I was speaking to him recently but when put to bed his temperature did not rise. He denies he ever had malaria. Sleeps and eats well'. Two weeks after admission, Corporal IJ was transferred to Belfast War Hospital for further treatment.

Melancholia or depression was a common problem in other war hospitals, too, and was the most common diagnosis (18 per cent) among soldiers from the expeditionary force in France admitted to the Lord Derby War Hospital, Warrington, Lancashire between June 1916 and June 1917.[29] Similar problems were reported from Dykebar War Hospital, Paisley where 21 per cent of admissions were labelled manic-depressive, of whom 71 per cent were predominantly depressive and 16 per cent predominantly excited or manic.[30] At the Welsh Metropolitan War Hospital, Whitchurch, Cardiff melancholia accounted for 19.6 per cent of admissions to the 'Mental Division' between September 1917 and September 1919.[31]

Suicidal behaviour was also a very real problem, although Henderson reported one case form Lord Derby War Hospital in which suicidal threats were used as a means to leave the army.[32] In addition, however, significant acts of deliberate self-harm were reported from Lord Derby War Hospital too,[33] and similar acts of self-harm were also recorded at the Richmond War Hospital, in combination with depressed mood.

In early 1919, for example, Private OP, a 37-year-old, Roman Catholic private, was admitted to the Richmond War Hospital, again from King George V Hospital. On admission, physical examination revealed that Private OP had a 'scar across neck of self-inflicted wound. He is fairly well-nourished'. Mentally, Private OP was 'dull, depressed and wears a despondent appearance. He complains of pain and noises in his head and says he imagines someone talks to him. He seems to be hypochondriacal and complains his health was broken down by malaria contracted in Salonica' (i.e. Thessaloniki in Greece, scene of a lengthy British campaign in the war).

Clinical notes on the day after admission stated that 'this man remained quiet and sleeps well during the night'. After one week at the War Hospital, Private OP 'was perhaps somewhat brighter in his manner but he still suffers from hallucinations of hearing and has vague persecutory delusions.... He sleeps and eats well'. Three weeks after admission, Private OP was, like Corporal IJ, 'transferred to Belfast War Hospital'. This was a common occurrence, as soldiers moved frequently within the network of hospitals established during the war,[34] sometimes for reasons related to soldiers' places of origin.

Diagnosing shell shock in soldiers during this period was a complex matter, not least owing to the difficulty of distinguishing 'true' cases from cases of malingering; the distinction was, according to some authorities, merely a question of the degree to which the wilfulness to be affected was conscious or subconscious.[35] What was clear to all, however, was the *extent* of the overall problem for the army, and the need for soldiers such as those admitted to the Richmond War Hospital to be restored to good health. Accurate descriptions of symptoms, such as those in the clinical records at the Richmond War Hospital, were clearly necessary in order to generate a diagnostic system which would help identify treatments and elucidate prognosis.

Today, the diagnosis most likely to be applied to many of these cases is 'post-traumatic stress disorder' (PTSD) which, according to the World Health Organisation (WHO) 'arises as a delayed and/or protracted response to a stressful event or situation (either short- or long-lasting) of an exceptionally threatening or catastrophic nature, which is likely to cause pervasive distress in almost anyone (for example, natural or man-made disaster, combat, serious accident, witnessing the violent death of others, or being the victim of torture, terrorism, rape, or other crime).'[36]

According to the current WHO conceptualisation of the disorder, PTSD must arise with six months of the traumatic event and may be characterised by a particular set of distressing symptoms, including re-enactment or recollection of the event through memories, dreams or other imagery; numbing of emotions and feelings; and avoidance of reminders of the traumatic event.[37] Other features may include mood problems, alterations in behaviour, hypervigilance (jumpiness), insomnia (poor sleep), anxiety and depression. Abuse of alcohol or other substances may also occur in time, sometimes in a futile effort to manage the core symptoms of PTSD.

As was the case with shell shock, different individuals may present with different constellations of symptoms, as outlined by the American Psychiatric Association in 2013:

> The clinical presentation of PTSD varies. In some individuals, fear-based re-experiencing, emotional, and behavioural symptoms may predominate. In others, anhedonic or dysphoric [i.e. low] mood states and negative cognitions [thoughts] may be most distressing. In some other individuals, arousal and reactive-externalizing symptoms are prominent, while in others, dissociative symptoms predominate. Finally, some individuals exhibit combinations of these symptoms patterns.[38]

While one must exercise great caution applying the diagnostic categories of today to cases from the past, it is relatively clear that many soldiers admitted to the Richmond War Hospital fulfilled at least some of the contemporary criteria for PTSD, including witnessing combat and the violent deaths of others, being exposed to shell fire, and presenting with symptoms highly consistent with both current descriptions of PTSD and the early twentieth-century accounts of shell shock. There was, however, one group of cases that presented a particular diagnostic challenge at the time, and these were soldiers who had been prisoners of war (POWs) and now presented with psychological symptoms, despite the widespread belief among certain clinicians of the day that being a POW actually *protected* soldiers from psychological problems, rather than caused them.

## The Psychological Effects of Being a Prisoner of War in the First World War

The psychological effects of being a POW were widely debated over the course of the twentieth century. By the end of the century, a considerable body of literature had accumulated to support the idea that being a POW, at least during the Second World War (1939–45) and Korean War (1950–53), could have enduring negative effects on mental health.[39] At the time of the First World War, however, when the Richmond War Hospital was in operation, this idea was far from accepted; indeed, it was widely believed spending time in captivity *protected* against mental illness. A psychiatric conference in Munich in September 1916, for example, examined the mental health of POWs concluded that they were immune from 'war neuroses' such as shell shock.[40]

While this position was not universally agreed,[41] it appeared to be backed up by evidence: one study of 12,000 French and British POWs in the First World War did not find a single case of neurosis, while another POW study reported just five cases among 80,000 POWs.[42] These conclusions are, however, significantly undermined by other sources of historical evidence, including evidence from British pension files which indicate that, after the war, large numbers of British POWs received financial compensation and suffered from psychological symptoms, such as neurasthenia or 'disordered action of the heart'[43] as a result of their experiences.[44]

The complexity of elucidating the precise effects of the POW experience is demonstrated by the case of Private FG, a 23-year-old, single Roman Catholic private, who was admitted to the Richmond War Hospital from King George V Hospital in 1919, having been 'a prisoner of war in Germany'. Private FG's admission notes record: 'Head very small. Degenerate in appearance. Weight: 9 stone, 6 pounds'.

The term 'degenerate' refers to the contemporary theory of 'degeneration' which held that mental illness was largely biological and genetic in origin, and was not only transmitted from generation to generation, but worsened with each generational cycle.[45] The theory of degeneration was popularised in the mid-1800s by Benedict-Augustin Morel (1809–73) in France. Morel also contended that mental illness was accompanied by particular physical features, such as the allegedly 'very small' head described in relation to Private FG. In the case of Private FG, the use of the term 'degenerate' may reflect the asylum officer's impression that Private FG suffered from pre-existing mental illness instead of, or in addition to, the psychological effects of war.

Mentally, admission notes describe Private FG as:

> ... very dull and unable to give a collected account of himself. His memory is very confused. He told me one time he was never out of Ireland. At another, he told me he was at the base in Italy.... He also stated he never carried a rifle and was never interested in musketry. He claims he has headaches at times and suffers from noises in his head. He is very feeble-minded. I have learned through King George V Hospital that he was a prisoner in Germany.... He claims he joined the army about 1½ or 2 years ago ... that he was drilled but never instructed in musketry.

One week after admission Private FG was 'still very dull and apathetic. His memory is very confused. He states he never left Ireland since he joined the army. Demented. Eats and sleeps well'. In relation to the term 'demented', it is important to note that, in the early twentieth-century, the meaning of the term 'dementia' differed from its contemporary meaning. In the early twentieth-century, 'dementia' was used to denote any severe mental disorder with delusions (fixed, false beliefs which are not amenable to reason) and/or hallucinations (perceptions without appropriate external stimuli), whereas currently the term generally refers to certain chronic brain syndromes chiefly seen in later life (for example, Alzheimer's disease). These changes in the use of psychiatric terminology over time add greatly to the difficulty in interpreting clinical diagnoses from the early twentieth century, and render it extremely difficult to establish systematically the contemporary equivalents of psychiatric disorders recorded in medical notes from that period.

In any case, two months after admission to the Richmond War Hospital, clinical records record that Private FG was still 'dull, apathetic, demented. Takes no interest in anything. He denies he was ever a prisoner of war but now admits he was working at the base in France. Has no idea of time. Sleeps and eats well'. Three months after admission he remained 'dull, apathetic, memory bad. Keeps to himself. Rather uncommunicative'. He remained in this state until at least five months after admission, at which point the medical record is abruptly and inexplicably terminated; it is likely he was transferred to either another war hospital or possibly the main Richmond Asylum itself.

While there is no further record of Private FG's clinical progress, his story indicates that at least some POWs were admitted to the Richmond War Hospital, although it is substantially less clear to what extent Private FG's symptoms were due to his POW experience, to what extent they stemmed from other experiences of war (for example, exposure to shell fire), and to what extent they were attributable to pre-existing mental illness. Efforts to elucidate these issues from the clinical records is complicated by the fact that the negative psychological effects of being a POW were not widely accepted at the time of the First World War[46] and, as a result, medical officers may have pro-actively sought other explanations for psychological symptoms such as those experienced by Private FG.

The generally benign view of the psychological effects of the POW experience around the time of the First World War was to change later in the twentieth century, when, after the Second World War, the negative effects of being a POW became significantly clearer. One of the clearest accounts of this was written by Dr Aidan McCarthy, who was born and grew up in Castletownbere, County Cork, and graduated as a medical doctor from University College Cork in 1938.[47] McCarthy joined the Royal Air Force (RAF) in 1939 and was held as a POW in Japan. After the war, McCarthy was awarded an OBE for his later POW work.

McCarthy's personal account of the POW experience in the Second World War is stark and disturbing: the food in the Japanese camps was 'appalling'; the accommodation 'badly overcrowded and soon bacillary dysentery cases appeared'; 'diabolical punishment' was performed on certain prisoners; and the forced labour was 'reminiscent of a Tractarian picture of Hell'.[48] Following his release, McCarthy was clearly in a state of 'shock':

> It is very difficult to describe my feelings at this time. I found it hard to believe that the brutality, beatings and starvation were over. I found it impossible to believe that the recent holocaust was real, not just a nightmare. Home seemed even less real. It was like being in a void. We lived for the day, neither able to look back into the past – nor look forward into the future. Later I realised that we must have been in a state of shock.[49]

Following the release of POWs after the Second World War, 'the Medical Branch of the RAF had a busy time rehabilitating minds and body to normality. The neuro-psychiatrists soon realised that their experiences with German POWs had not prepared them for the Far East POWs at all'.[50] Clearly, the POW experience in the Second World War had substantial potential to produce adverse psychological effects, and the case of Private FG at the Richmond War Hospital, combined with other historical evidence from First World War pension files,[51] suggests psychological trauma of a similar nature among at least some POWs from the First World War too, although its precise parameters are difficult to define.

Overall, the soldiers admitted to the Richmond War Hospital presented with a wide variety of symptoms, many of which accorded with contemporary clinical descriptions of shell shock, commonly combined with substantial levels of depression. This diversity of clinical presentations was not unique to the Richmond. In 1917, at the spring meeting of the Irish Division of the MPA, which discussed the Richmond War Hospital in some detail,[52] Major W.R. Dawson, 'Specialist in Nerve Diseases to the Troops in Ireland',[53] emphasised the variety of clinical presentations of shell shock:

> Major WR Dawson gave a most interesting account of cases of shell shock and cases resulting from war stress. These varied from cases of slight nervous disturbance, where men were easily startled by sudden sounds or noises, to the most serious breakdowns.
>
> Cases in which excessive tremor was a cardinal symptom in patients suffering from traumatic neurasthenia, loss of speech, and hearing, and sight. Loss of sight appeared to be regained quicker than the loss of hearing or speech. It is often most difficult to restore the powers of speech. Some had got good results from treatment by hypnotism, but this

had been found of little use in other hands. Major Dawson spoke of the great kindness and attention of Dr Forde and Dr Dwyer [at the Richmond War Hospital] with regard to the wounded soldiers, which was beyond all praise.[54]

One of the most interesting features of many of the cases at the Richmond War Hospital was the fact that many appeared to experience substantial reductions in symptoms during their relatively short time there. Gunner GH, for example, was 'much improved' after just four weeks in the War Hospital and was discharged three weeks later. Private JK had 'improved considerably' after a single week and Gunner MN was 'very much improved in every way' after a fortnight. This rate of recovery and discharge was by no means unique to the Richmond War Hospital: at Lord Derby War Hospital in Lancashire, some 30 per cent of admissions were categorised under the heading of 'mental deficiency' but their acute symptoms were 'of an exceedingly transitory nature', so the average period these patients spent in the hospital was approximately six weeks.[55]

What was responsible for these apparently remarkable transformations of soldiers who arrived crippled with shell shock and depression, and were discharged a few short weeks later, apparently recovered? The therapeutic approach to shell shock and other mental troubles resulting from war, and the treatments used at the Richmond War Hospital in particular, are considered next.

## Endnotes

[1] Myers, C.S., 'A contribution to the study of shell shock'. *Lancet* 1915; 185: 316-20; Myers, C.S., 'Contributions to the study of shell shock: Being an account of certain disorders of cutaneous sensibility'. *Lancet* 1916; 187: 608-13; Rivers, W.H.R., *Instinct and the Unconscious: A Contribution to a Biological Theory of the Psycho-Neuroses*. Cambridge: Cambridge University Press, 1920; Shepherd, B., *A War of Nerves: Soldiers and Psychiatrists, 1914-1994*. London: Pimlico, 2002.

[2] Walsh, D., 'The ups and downs of schizophrenia in Ireland'. *Irish Journal of Psychiatry* 1992; 13: 12-6.

[3] Bartlett, P., *The Poor Law of Lunacy*. London and Washington: Leicester University Press, 1999; p. 159.

[4] Porter, R., 'The patient's view. Doing medical history from below'. *Theory and Society* 1985; 14: 175-98; p. 175.

[5] Smith, L., "Your very thankful inmate': Discovering the patients of an early county lunatic asylum'. *Social History of Medicine* 2008; 21: 237-52.

[6] Risse, G.B., Warner, J.H., 'Reconstructing clinical activities: Patient records in medical history'. *Social History of Medicine* 1992; 5: 183-205; p. 183.

[7] The Act of Union of 1 January 1801 declared Ireland to be part of the United Kingdom of Great Britain and Ireland. The twenty-six counties that now comprise the Republic of Ireland were declared a republic in 1949.

[8] Howorth, P., 'The treatment of shell shock: Cognitive therapy before its time'. *Psychiatric Bulletin* 2000; 24: 225-7; p. 225. See also: Merskey, H., *The Analysis of Hysteria*. London: Gaskell, 1979.

[9] Jones, E., Wessely, S., *Shell Shock to PTSD: Military Psychiatry from 1900 to the Gulf War* (Maudsley Monographs 47). East Sussex, UK: Psychology Press (Taylor & Francis Group) on behalf of The Maudsley, 2005.

[10] Jones, E., 'Historical approaches to post-combat disorders'. *Philosophical Transactions of the Royal Society* B 2006; 361: 533-42; p. 534.

[11] Erichsen, J.E., *On Railway and Other Injuries of the Nervous System*. Philadelphia: Henry C. Lea, 1867.

[12] Murray, L.M., 'The common factor in disordered action of the heart'. *British Medical Journal* 1918; 2(3024): 650-2; p. 650.

[13] Jones, E., 'Historical approaches to post-combat disorders'. *Philosophical Transactions of the Royal Society* B 2006; 361: 533-42; p. 534.

[14] Ibid, p. 535.

[15] Ibid, p. 537.

[16] Mitchell, T.J., Smith, G.M., *Medical Services, Casualties, and Medical Statistics of the Great War*. London: His Majesty's Stationery Office, 1931.

[17] Salmon, T.W., 'The care and treatment of mental diseases and war neuroses ('shell shock') in the British army'. *Mental Hygiene* 1917; 1: 509–47.

[18] Johnson, W., Rows, R.G., 'Neurasthenia and war neuroses'. In: MacPherson, W.G., Herringham, W.P., Elliott, T.R., Balfour, A. (eds), *History of the Great War Based on Official Documents, Volume II: Medical Services, Diseases of War* (pp. 1-67). London: HMSO, 1923.

[19] Collins, A. 'The Richmond District Asylum and the 1916 Easter Rising'. *Irish Journal of Psychological Medicine* 2013; 30: 279-83.

[20] Myers, C.S., 'A contribution to the study of shell shock'. *Lancet* 1915; 185: 316-20.

[21] Myers, C.S., 'Contributions to the study of shell shock: Being an account of certain disorders of cutaneous sensibility'. *Lancet* 1916; 187: 608-13.

[22] *The Irish Times*, for example, reported about shell shock in 1916, in connection with 'the fighting at Ypres' (*Irish Times*, 12 June 1916). See also: 'Ireland's Roll of Honour' (*Irish Times*, 23 September 1916) and 'A Grand Red Cross Fete & Horse-Jumping Competition' (*Irish Times*, 9 August 1917).

[23] Howorth, P., 'The treatment of shell shock: Cognitive therapy before its time'. *Psychiatric Bulletin* 2000; 24: 225-7. For further details on many of these hospitals, see: Jones and Wessely, *Shell Shock to PTSD*.

[24] Eager, R., 'A record of admissions to the mental section of the Lord Derby War Hospital, Warrington, from June 17th, 1916 to June 16th, 1917'. *Journal of Mental Science* 1918; 64: 272-96.

[25] Mott, F.W., 'Special discussion on shell shock without visible signs of injury'. *Proceedings of the Royal Society of Medicine* 1916; 9: i–xxiv; Mott, F.W., 'The microscopic examination of the brains of two men dead of commotion cerebri (shell shock) without visible external injury'. *British Medical Journal* 1917; 2: 612–5.

[26] Myers, C.S., 'A contribution to the study of shell shock'. *Lancet* 1915; 185: 316-20; Salmon, T.W., 'The care and treatment of mental diseases and war neuroses ('shell shock') in the British army'. *Mental Hygiene* 1917; 1: 509–47.

[27] Elliot Smith, G., Pear, T.H., *Shell Shock and its Lessons*. London: Longmans, Green & Co., 1917; pp. 6, 7.

[28] See *The Irish Times* (11 October 1918) in relation to the treatment of shell shock at the Hermitage, Lucan, which reportedly achieved 'excellent results' in such cases; see also: 'A Grand Red Cross Fete & Horse-Jumping Competition' (*Irish Times*, 9 August 1917).

[29] Eager, R., 'A record of admissions to the mental section of the Lord Derby War Hospital, Warrington, from June 17th, 1916 to June 16th, 1917.' *Journal of Mental Science* 1918; 64: 272-96; p. 282.

[30] Hotchkis, R.D., 'Renfrew District Asylum as a war hospital for mental invalids: some contrasts in administration with an analysis of cases admitted during the first year.' *Journal of Mental Science* 1917; 63: 238-49; p. 244.

[31] Barton White, E., 'Abstract of a report on the mental division of the Welsh Metropolitan War Hospital, Whitchurch, Cardiff, September, 1917-September, 1919.' *Journal of Mental Science* 1920; 66: 438-49; p. 442.

[32] Henderson, D.K., 'War psychoses: An analysis of 202 cases of mental disorder occurring in home troops.' *Journal of Mental Science* 1918; 64: 165-89; p. 171. For a discussion of insubordination, see: Eager, R., 'A record of admissions to the mental section of the Lord Derby War Hospital, Warrington, from June 17th, 1916 to June 16th, 1917.' *Journal of Mental Science* 1918; 64: 272-96; p. 291.

[33] Ibid.

[34] For further details on many of these hospitals, see: Jones and Wessely, *Shell Shock to PTSD*.

[35] Shepherd, *A War of Nerves*; p. 114.

[36] This passage is reproduced, with the permission of the publisher, from World Health Organisation. *The ICD-10 Classification of Mental and Behavioural Disorders: Clinical Descriptions and Diagnostic Guidelines.* Geneva: World Health Organisation, 1992; p. 147.

[37] Ibid, pp. 148-9.

[38] American Psychiatric Association. *Diagnostic and Statistical Manual of Mental Disorders (5th edition).* Washington DC: American Psychiatric Association, 2013; p. 274.

[39] Page, W.F., *The Health of Former Prisoners of War: Results from the Medical Examination Survey of Former POWs of World War II and the Korean Conflict.* Washington DC: National Academy Press, 1992.

[40] Jones, E., Wessely, S., 'British prisoners-of-war: From resilience to psychological vulnerability: Reality or perception'. *Twentieth Century British History* 2010; 21: 163-83; p. 164.

[41] Barton White, E., 'Abstract of a report on the mental division of the Welsh Metropolitan War Hospital, Whitchurch, Cardiff, September, 1917-September, 1919'. *Journal of Mental Science* 1920; 66: 438-49; p. 438.

[42] Lerner, P., 'From traumatic neurosis to male hysteria: The decline and fall of Hermann Oppenheim, 1889-1919'. In: Micale, M., Lerner, P. (eds), *Traumatic Pasts: History, Psychiatry and Trauma in the Modern Age, 1870–1930* (pp. 140-71). Cambridge: Cambridge University 2001.

[43] Jones, E., Hodgins Vermaas, R., McCartney, H., Everitt, B., Beech, C., Poynter, D., Palmer, I., Hyams, K., Wessely, S. 'Post-combat syndromes from the Boer War to the Gulf: A cluster analysis of their nature and attribution'. *British Medical Journal* 2002; 324: 321–4; Jones and Wessely, *Shell Shock to PTSD*.

[44] Jones, E., Wessely, S., 'British prisoners-of-war: From resilience to psychological vulnerability: Reality or perception'. *Twentieth Century British History* 2010; 21: 163-83; p. 166.

[45] Shorter, E., *A History of Psychiatry: From the Era of the Asylum to the Age of Prozac*. New York: John Wiley and Sons, 1997; pp. 93-4.

[46] Jones, E., Wessely, S., 'British prisoners-of-war: From resilience to psychological vulnerability: Reality or perception'. *Twentieth Century British History* 2010; 21: 163-83; p. 166.

[47] McCarthy, A., *A Doctor's War*. Cork: The Collins Press, 2005.

[48] Ibid, p. 104. The term 'Tractarian' refers to the teachings of the 'Oxford Movement', a movement of High Church Anglicans in Great Britain, which argued in favour of the reinstatement of various Christian traditions of faith and their incorporation into Anglican liturgy and theology.

[49] Ibid, p. 139.

[50] Ibid, p. 158.

[51] Jones, E,, Wessely, S., 'British prisoners-of-war: From resilience to psychological vulnerability: Reality or perception'. *Twentieth Century British History* 2010; 21: 163-83; p. 166.

[52] Anonymous. Irish Division. *Journal of Mental Science* 1917; 63: 297-9.

[53] Dawson, W.R., 'The work of the Belfast War Hospital (1917-1919)'. *Journal of Mental Science* 1925; 71: 219-24; p. 219.

[54] Anonymous. Irish Division. *Journal of Mental Science* 1917; 63: 297-9; p. 299.

[55] Henderson, D.K., 'War psychoses: An analysis of 202 cases of mental disorder occurring in home troops'. *Journal of Mental Science* 1918; 64: 165-89; p. 166.

# 4

# 'Rest of Mind and Body': Treatment at the Richmond War Hospital

As the diagnosis of shell shock became increasingly common, a broad range of treatments were proposed. The nature of these treatments reflected diverse views about the origins of shell shock as well as differing opinions about the best way to resolve its debilitating symptoms.

Some of the initial treatments for shell shock were notably disciplinary in nature, highlighting an apparent conflict between private intentions of the soldier and a sense of public duty, leading to the use of isolation, restricted diet and even electric shocks to alter soldiers' behaviour.[1] Other treatments were more psychological in nature, regarding war neurosis as attributable, at least in part, to unconscious psychological conflict in the soldier's mind. This idea led to treatments such as hypnosis and abreaction, which involved soldiers re-experiencing or re-living traumatic memories in an effort to purge them of their emotional impact. In all cases, there was a strong emphasis on prompt treatment, cognitive re-structuring of the traumatic experiences, (that is, thinking about them differently)[2] and collaboration with the therapist in the search for a cure. Many of these therapies have certain similarities with current cognitive and behavioural approaches to PTSD, focussing on altering patterns of thought and behaviour so as to reduce symptoms.[3]

There were, however, other approaches to the management of shell shock which certain authorities viewed as equally if not more effective than approaches based on discipline, hypnosis, re-experiencing or abreaction. These included, most notably, approaches based primarily on rest and less intrusive forms of therapy.[4] Against the background of this controversy, this chapter explores the therapeutic approaches used at the Richmond War Hospital and pays particular attention to the provision of rest and quietude for soldiers, as well as care for physical illnesses such as epilepsy and malaria.

## 'The Quietness of This Place': Treating Shell Shock at the Richmond War Hospital

After the First World War had ended, the War Office, in 1922, published its comprehensive *Report of the War Office Committee of Enquiry into 'Shell-Shock'*.[5] The report was a collection and distillation of clinical and military expertise in shell shock gained during the First World War and its aftermath. In the course of its deliberations, the Committee heard evidence from a broad range of experts about the causes and treatments for shell shock. Many drew attention to the importance of rest in preventing shell shock in the first instance:

> Captain Gee, V.C., expressed himself emphatically that frequent leave home did much to prevent nervous breakdown, and attributed the comparative absence of 'shell-shock' in his brigade to this. He also advocated rest in cases showing initial symptoms of nervous breakdown.

> Colonel Fuller considered that if organisation, training and administration were based on a psychological foundation, 'shell-shock' and nervous strain could be combated, and considered that in training insufficient regard was given to

the psychology of the individual. A high morale undoubtedly tended to lessen 'shell-shock'. Morale depended chiefly on a sense of security and comfort. Officers should be assiduous in their concern for their men. Removal from the front and visits home lessen the incidence of 'shell-shock'.

Dr Mapother thought every anxiety neurosis case in its very early stage could have been cured if taken out of the line and sent to a rest camp.[6]

In its final recommendations, the Committee warned against the indiscriminate use of therapies based on discipline, hypnosis, re-experiencing or abreaction:

> The committee are of opinion that the production of hypnoidal state and deep hypnotic sleep, while beneficial as a means of conveying suggestions or eliciting forgotten experiences are useful in selected cases, but in the majority they are unnecessary and may even aggravate the symptoms for a time. They do not recommend psycho-analysis in the Freudian sense.[7]

Instead, the Committee placed strong emphasis on the curative properties of simple 'rest of mind and body':

> The establishment of an atmosphere of cure is the basis of all successful treatment, the personality of the physician is, therefore, of the greatest importance. While recognising that each individual case of war neurosis must be treated on its merits, the Committee are of opinion that good results will be obtained in the majority by the simplest forms of psycho-therapy, i.e., explanation, persuasion and suggestion, aided by such physical methods as baths, electricity and massage. Rest of mind and body is essential in all cases.[8]

This approach, based primarily on rest and recuperation, is in plentiful evidence in the records of the Richmond War

Hospital. Private HI, for example, was a 25-year-old, single, Roman Catholic private admitted to the Richmond War Hospital in 1918 owing to the 'hardship and stress of [the] Campaign'. On admission, Private HI was 'nervous and slightly irritable and inclined to be voluble and has vague persecutory delusions. He complains of headache and noises in his head like bells and often thinks he hears people calling him. He complains of troublesome dreams of death and murder, and states he is easily excited and then loses control of himself even if not implicated in what would excite him, such as a row among other men'.

Private HI had joined the army in 1913 and gone to the Front in 1914. He returned in early 1918, 'suffering from otitis media [inflammation of the ear], nervous debility and shock'. On his first night at the Richmond War Hospital, Private HI 'remained quiet and slept well during the night'. One week after admission, he was 'very quiet and well-conducted. He still complains of pain in his head occasionally but states he has much improved owing to the quietness of this place. He seems to be quite rational at present. Sleeps and eats well. '

Two weeks after admission, Private HI was 'very quiet and well-conducted. He states he is feeling better now than he thought he would ever be in his life, He states his head is very well at present. Sleeps and eats well'. Three weeks later, after five weeks in the Richmond War Hospital, Private HI was discharged.

Not all patients remained 'quiet and well-conducted' during their time at the War Hospital; some required transfer to the main Richmond District Asylum, where a minority remained for extended periods. Private PQ, for example, was a 21-year-old Roman Catholic private admitted to the Richmond War Hospital from another war hospital in Wales in late 1918. On physical examination, Private PQ's tongue was 'tremulous. Pupils large ...

Left arm more or less disabled. Scar on left shoulder'. Mentally, 'he has hallucinations of sight. He tells me he sees the Germans everywhere he goes if he gets excited and that he hears noises at times but never hears voices. States he loses the sight of his eyes at times. He seems somewhat weak-minded'.

During his first night at the Richmond War Hospital, Private PQ 'remained quiet and slept well during the night'. One week after admission, clinical notes record that 'this man became quarrelsome and violent a few days ago and fought with another patient. He had to be moved to the observation ward. He is rather nervous and excitable. He sleeps and eats well'.

Two weeks after admission, matters had improved considerably: 'He has calmed down very much and is now back in the [War] Hospital. He states he is feeling much better now and is not subject so much to the noises and headaches, and that he feels generally improved since he came here. He is very much quieter and more rational in his conduct. Sleeps and eats well'.

One month after admission, Private PQ was 'very much improved. He is now very quiet and well-conducted and gives no trouble. He expresses no delusion. He is allowed out every day'. Two months after admission he remained 'very much improved, bodily and mentally. He is very quiet and well-conducted. He expresses no delusion. Denies headache, hallucinations. Sleeps and eats well'.

Three months after admission, Private PQ was 'now rational in his conversation. He is very quiet and gives no trouble. Sleeps and eats well'. Three weeks later, after three-and-a-half months in the War Hospital, Private PQ was discharged to the care of his wife.

In addition to the 'quietness of this place', from which Privates HI and PQ apparently benefitted, the Richmond War Hospital offered other forms of psycho-social support for the soldiers, at least some of which were, as Reynolds points out, attributable 'the cooperation and involvement of voluntary organisations in the care of the patients':

> The Irish Automobile Club took patients out for drives. In his annual report for 1916, [RMS] Donelan thanked the Irish Automobile Club, the Irish Red Cross Society, Colonel W.R. Dawson, the Royal Artillery Medical Corps and others for their generous assistance towards the recreation and comfort of the patients. Although singers and dramatic groups had visited the asylum in the past and had entertained the patients, the involvement of the voluntary groups with the war hospital was more regular and sustained.[9]

The Red Cross was very involved in the management of shell shock in Dublin[10] and the *Richmond War Hospital Admission and Discharge Book* notes rather sternly that all 'shell shock cases [were] to be notified' to the 'American Red Cross, Rathfarnham'.[11]

As well as outings, singers and dramatic groups, there were also 'games' in the War Hospital, and participation in games was seen as a clear indicator of recovery, consistent with the strong emphasis that many asylums, including the Richmond,[12] placed on sport and related activities.[13] Private LM, for example, was a 23-year-old, single, Roman Catholic private who presented to the Richmond War Hospital in late 1918 from a military barracks in Dublin. He was accompanied by a paper stating: 'This man reported here and is unable to give an account of himself. I have instructed him to be taken to hospital'. On admission, Private LM was 'stout, strong, healthy-looking. Heart and lungs clear. Small toes override the ones next. Mid-finger of right hand amputated from root'.

Mentally, Private LM was 'dull and confused but wears an air of importance out of keeping with his position. His memory is very bad. He states he belongs to the 'Secret Society', the 'Intelligent Department', and goes on to say he was appointed by the Lord Lieutenant [the chief administrator of government in Ireland] yesterday'. He 'states he met him [the Lord Lieutenant] outside somewhere near this place yet he does not know where he is. He states he has some pain in his head and also hears some noises and hears people speak by wireless code telling him to have a sharp look out'. He 'denied drinking'.

Private LM could recall few details about his service in the army except that he had been in Canada. He didn't 'remember where he was stationed last. Says he 'was on guard last night at that barracks' but does not know the name of it'. It appears that Private LM had called to an army barracks in Dublin the previous night 'and asked the men on guard for the Intelligence Officer and stated he wanted to see him. He got placed in the guard room for the night'. The following day, Private LM was sent to the Richmond War Hospital for assessment and treatment.

On the day after admission, Private LM 'remained quiet and slept well. His memory is still confused'. Three days later, however, Private LM was 'fairly bright and cheerful' and remembered more details of his military service. In addition, 'he has now lost all his silly ideas about the service. Sleeps and eats well'. Two weeks after admission, Private LM was 'much improved. He is bright and cheerful and joins in games and gives no trouble. Sleeps and eats well'. One month after admission, Private LM was 'now quite normal and seems rational'. Three weeks later, he was discharged from the Richmond War Hospital and 'removed to the Canadian Depot in England'.

## Medicinal Treatments at the Hospital

In addition to the 'quietness of this place' that benefited Privates HI and PQ, and the 'games' and recreation in which Private LM participated, staff at the Richmond War Hospital also used various medicinal treatments, as outlined at the spring meeting of the Irish Division of the Medico Psychological Association of Great Britain and Ireland (MPA), which was held in Dublin on 5 April 1917.[14] The MPA was a continuation of the Association of Medical Officers of Asylums and Hospitals for the Insane which was founded in 1841 by Dr Samuel Hitch (1800–81), resident superintendent of the Gloucestershire General Lunatic Asylum.[15] The purpose of the organisation was to facilitate communication between doctors working in asylums with a view to improving quality of care provided to the mentally ill. In 1887 the organisation's name was changed to the Medico Psychological Association of Great Britain and Ireland (MPA) and in 1894 it admitted its first woman member, Dr Eleonora Fleury of the Richmond Asylum.[16]

At the spring 1917 meeting of the Irish Division of the MPA, Donelan, RMS of the Richmond, 'gave a most interesting account of the War Hospital work of the Richmond Asylum'.[17] At that point, the War Hospital had been in operation for ten months and had admitted 104 cases 'suffering from mental trouble due to three varieties of causation'; these included:

> (1) Patients who would have become insane in all probability in any case, having had previous attacks before the war; (2) patients with neurotic constitutions whose resistance to stress and war conditions was insufficient to ensure their remaining free from mental trouble; (3) patients whose condition was directly due to shell shock and stress of war conditions. These cases of shell shock were usually merely confusional insanity passing into stupor, often of particular faculties.[18]

A wide variety of treatments was in use:

Dr Forde, who had had many opportunities of treating these cases, gave the meeting the benefit of his experiences. He regarded these cases of shell shock as due to a dislocation of the brain-cells. Hot and cold baths given alternately had produced good results in some cases of loss of the power of speech. Many cases are borderland cases of insanity. There was marked tremulousness of the musculature and shakings of the body, with profuse perspiration of the skin of the head. He had found a mixture of the bromides, together with antipyrin, and citrate of caffeine, gave great relief where headaches existed, and when the mixture was discontinued the men begged for its repetition. Fletcher's syrup of the hydrobromates was useful, and hastened recovery in some of the cases he had treated.[19]

Many of these treatments were long-established treatments that were already in use at the Richmond District Asylum and elsewhere. The 'hot and cold baths' to which Forde referred were a continuation of the long-standing practice of hydrotherapy (regular shower-baths, etc.),[20] which would later be recommended for shell shock in the 1922 *Report of the War Office Committee of Enquiry into 'Shell-Shock'*.[21]

Antipyrin, also known as phenazone, is an analgesic, non-steroidal anti-inflammatory and antipyretic medication (i.e. reduces pain and body temperature) that was first discovered in 1883 by Ludwig Knorr (1859–1921), a German chemist.[22] Its actions in alleviating pain, reducing inflammation and restoring body temperature would have been very useful for soldiers suffering the after-effects of battle.

Caffeine, too, was used by Forde at the Richmond War Hospital and was the subject of approving mention in Dr William H. Burt's 1896 edition of *Physiological Materia Medica (Containing All that is Known of the Physiological Action of Our*

*Remedies Together with their Characteristic Indications and Pharmacology)*:

> Caffeine is a marked diuretic, from its great power to increase the renal arterial blood-pressure.... Citrate of Caffeine has been found to possess great value as a diuretic and cardiac stimulant.... Caffeine checks and lessens the elimination of nitrogen by diminishing the amount of urea excreted, and, in this way, is of great service to man in preventing the tissue metamorphosis, or actual wear and tear, of daily life.[23]

The addictive potential of caffeine was clearly recognised at the Richmond as Forde noted that 'when the mixture was discontinued the men begged for its repetition'. Bromides, also used by Forde at the War Hospital, also had a chequered history in psychiatry, having been used to induce 'bromide sleep' towards the end of the 1800s, but then abandoned, possibly owing to toxicity.[24] Fletcher's hydrobromate syrup, specifically recommended by Forde, was a curious concoction, listed in the *British Medical Journal* on 1 April 1882 in its 'Reports and Analyses and Descriptions of New Inventions in Medicine, Surgery, Dietetics and the Allied Sciences':

> *Fletcher and Fletcher's Syrup of Hydrobromate of Iron and Quinine.* This is by no means an unpalatable preparation, and affords a convenient mode of administering a useful remedy. Each fluid drachm contains two grains of hydrobromate of iron, one grain of hydrobromate of quinine, with thirty minims of dilute hydrobromic acid. The dose is a teaspoonful or more in water.[25]

Soon after its appearance, Fletcher's hydrobromate syrup was a widely used remedy for, among other ailments, 'exhaustion of the brain',[26] and it clearly formed an important part of the complex mixture of medicines administered by Forde and colleagues at the Richmond War Hospital in 1917.

The treatments described by Forde were not, however, the only possible treatment options at the time. Other approaches included 'treatment in country houses', as was practiced in England, based primarily on rest and recuperation,[27] and administration of phosferine, which claimed to be a 'proven remedy for influenza, nervous debility, indigestion' and some seventeen other ailments, including 'mental exhaustion' and 'nerve shock'.[28] Phosferine, which is a herbal supplement containing cinchona bark extract, was, according to its advertisement, recommended by 'ES Eslam' of the 'British Expeditionary Force' who 'realises that it is entirely due to phosferine he owes his recovery from nervous breakdown – phosferine replenished his system with the vital force to regain its former energy and power of resistance'. Notwithstanding these apparently miraculous powers, and the detailed testimony of 'ES Eslam', there is no record that phosferine was used at the Richmond War Hospital.

In any case, after outlining the treatments provided at the hospital, Forde went on to provide the 1917 MPA meeting with an overview of cases seen at the Richmond War Hospital up to that point, during the first ten months of its operations:

> Hallucinations of sight and hearing were sometimes present, but many of the cases were quite conscious of the hallucinations, and realised that they were abnormal, and were, therefore, not to be regarded as ordinarily insane patients suffering from hallucinatory states. Altogether it appeared that 56 patients out of the original 104 had been dealt with at the Richmond Asylum War Hospital. Of these 26 had been sent to other asylums, 12 had been sent home, and the balance had been able to resume their occupations. The patients were segregated from the other asylum inmates, and not certified insane.[29]

In the ensuing discussion at the MPA meeting, Dr Leeper, honorary secretary of the MPA's Irish Division, who would later go on to become MPA president in 1931,[30] 'pointed out that so far as he understood the causation of shell shock was due to the sudden effect upon the blood vascular system by shell explosion, driving the blood of the body towards the nerve centres, and thereby disorganising or injuring them with sudden violence, or interfering with their functions.'[31] Whatever their causes, however, shell shock and mental troubles were not the only ailments among soldiers returning from war to the Richmond War Hospital; many had physical illnesses too, and these also presented significant challenges to patients and staff alike.

## Physical Illnesses in Soldiers at the Hospital

In addition to the mental troubles presented by soldiers presenting to the Richmond War Hospital, staff at the hospital also had to deal with physical illnesses among soldiers returning from the Front. All of the Irish asylums had already experienced significant difficulties with physical illnesses among inpatients in the decades leading up to the First World War. In the main Richmond District Asylum there was a particular problem with infectious diseases such as dysentery which, according to the Inspector of Lunatics in 1892, had become 'almost endemic in this institution – 73 cases with 14 deaths occurred last year, and it may be mentioned that in no less than three of these cases secondary abscesses were found in the liver.'[32] The death rate at the Richmond was, as a result, quite high, at 12.5 per cent per year, although similar rates were reported in asylums elsewhere; for example, South Carolina Lunatic Asylum which reported a death rate of 14 per cent, between 1890 and 1915.[33]

In 1915, the Inspectors of Lunatics expressed concern at the level of illness in the Richmond asylum generally:

This institution continues to be maintained in excellent order. There was, however, as usual, a considerable number of casualties and of cases of zymotic disease [acute, infectious diseases] during the year, the latter including dysentery [inflammation of the bowel], erysipelas [a skin infection], and enteric fever [associated with contaminated food or water]. A new sanitary block has been erected at the male exercise ground.[34]

These concerns persisted during the years when the Richmond War Hospital operated, although the death rate fell to 7.6% in 1917.[35] There had been a particularly significant problem with tuberculosis (TB)[36] which was the single most common cause of death among inpatients in the Irish psychiatric hospitals toward the end of the 1800s.[37] By the early 1900s, TB accounted for over 25 per cent of deaths in Irish mental hospitals[38] and almost 16 per cent of all deaths in the Irish population.[39] Similar problems were reported in asylums in other countries.[40] At the Richmond in 1907, the RMS, Dr John Conolly Norman,[41] drew the urgent attention of Richmond Asylum Joint Committee to the problem and recommended physical isolation of TB patients:

I believe the desirability of isolation as far as possible in cases of pulmonary consumption will now be generally recognised... The present, therefore, seems to be a particularly suitable time to again draw attention to the great prevalence among our patients of tuberculosis consumption and the need that exists for some special provision for isolating sufferers from this disease. No large scheme of new construction or re-arrangement ought to be considered without a special view to this topic.[42]

In due course, TB presented significant problems at the war hospitals of the First World War too,[43] where it was joined by a range of other infectious disorders as soldiers with a wide vari-

73

ety of physical illnesses, in addition to mental troubles, were admitted. Private CD, for example, was a Roman Catholic private admitted to the Richmond War Hospital in late 1918, having come directly from another war hospital in England. On admission Private CD's 'tongue and limbs were fairly steady' but he was mentally 'dull and mildly depressed and seems more-or-less despondent. He complains of some pain in his head and loss of memory. He states he used to hear some noise but this is now less troublesome and that at one time he thought he heard voices but these have also disappeared'. Private CD had been in the army for four years and served in the Dardanelles, Serbia, Macedonia, Egypt and Salonica.

One week after admission, medical records note that Private CD had 'a slight attack of malaria [from which he had suffered in the past] a couple of days ago and complained of some headache. He has been on quinine since'. Quinine was a standard treatment for malaria, which was a substantial problem among Irish soldiers in the war.[44] Two weeks after admission, Private CD was 'much improved. His headache has disappeared. He is, however, not quite as bright as one would wish. He sleeps and eats well'.

One month after admission, clinical notes record that Private CD was 'quiet but rather distant in his manner. He is very 'feeble-minded' ... he tried to step-dance [and] sing ... on invitation from his comrades. He has not the slightest idea of either'. He was, nonetheless, 'much improved'. Three months after admission, Private CD 'went out on pass'; 'took some drink'; and 'kicked up a row' at another Dublin hospital, He was 'brought back under escort'. The final opinion expressed about Private CD in the clinical records is that he was 'very feeble-minded and has little intelligence'. He was 'discharged to care of friends' just over four months after admission.

Malaria was a problem not only at the Richmond War Hospital but also at various other war hospitals, including the Welsh Metropolitan War Hospital in Cardiff, where malaria was identified as one of the most common factors contributing to nervous problems among soldiers.[45] For soldiers like Private CD, however, there were many factors relevant to their hospitalisation, including psychological symptoms ('pain in his head and loss of memory'; hearing 'noises' and 'voices'), physical illness (malaria) and possible pre-existing mental disorder ('very feeble-minded and has little intelligence'). On this basis, Private CD may have belonged to any or all of the three categories of patients identified by Donelan at the MPA meeting in spring 1917: '(1) Patients who would have become insane in all probability in any case, having had previous attacks'; '(2) patients with neurotic constitutions whose resistance to stress and war conditions was insufficient'; and '(3) patients whose condition was directly due to ... stress of war conditions'.[46]

Other physical illnesses impinged on these patients too. Private DE, for example, was a 27-year-old, Roman Catholic private admitted in 1918 owing to the 'stress of campaign'. He has previously been in Belfast War Hospital and King George V Hospital, Dublin. On admission to the Richmond War Hospital, Private DE's tongue was 'tremulous' and his right arm 'tremulous (fine) when extended'. Mentally, he was 'dull and depressed, sullen and morose. He complains of pain and noises in his head and states he hears voices sometimes but does not know what they say. He states he joined the army over three years ago and went to the front in France sometime in 1915'.

The admitting officer at the Richmond War Hospital recorded that Private DE was 'perspiring over the front part of his head. The orderly who accompanied him tells me he was very violent last night in George V Hospital'. At the Richmond, however, Private DE 'remained quiet and slept well'. One week after admission, Private DE was 'still depressed but shows some signs of brightening up. He still complains of headache. His tongue is tremulous but his limbs are fairly steady. He states he got mountain fever while in Italy and bled form the nose. He was sent to a mental hospital for a short time and was then sent on to France' for a short time. Ultimately, he was admitted to Belfast War Hospital after which he came to Dublin where he again 'got bad' and was admitted to the Richmond War Hospital.

Two weeks after admission, Private DE was 'still dull and mildly depressed' but was 'beginning to brighten up. He is much more communicative. He admits he is much better and that his head does not trouble him so much'. Two months after admission, Private DE was 'fairly bright and cheerful. He states he is feeling much better than he was. He expressed no definite delusion. Sleeps and eats well'. The following month he was still 'fairly bright and cheerful. Joins in games. States he is feeling well'. Four-and-a-half months after admission, Private DE was discharged to the care of his sister.

Private DE clearly had complex history of hospitalisation prior to his arrival at the Richmond War Hospital, having spent time in Belfast War Hospital, King George V Hospital (Dublin) and 'a mental hospital' in Italy. The 'mountain fever' from which he suffered was just one of a number of physical illnesses with which military medical personnel had to cope during the First World War; 'trench fever', first reported among the British forces in Flanders in 1915, and various other apparently infectious disorders, also presented significant challenges at the Front.[47] Other, non-infectious disorders were also in clear evidence both in the battlefield and, in due course, in the war hospitals, and presented similar challenges. Clinical records at the Richmond War Hospital contain especially compelling clinical descriptions of epilepsy, such as those provided in the records of Sergeant EF and Private QR.

## Epilepsy at the Richmond War Hospital

Sergeant EF, a 33-year-old Presbyterian, was admitted to the Richmond War Hospital from another Irish military hospital in 1918. Sergeant EF had a documented history of epilepsy having 'had a fit while in France. States he has been gradually losing the power of his left arm. This arm was injured in the African (Boer) War'.

On admission, Sergeant EF was 'fairly well nourished ... Tongue tremulous. Left arm weak in grasp. Scars above elbow ... States the loss of power has been gradual'. Mentally, Sergeant EF was 'fairly bright and cheerful' but 'complains of pain in his head. States he feels nervous and suffers from insomnia. He denies hallucinations'.

One week after admission, Sergeant EF had 'improved in his appearance and is bright and cheerful. He admits he is feeling better. He is sleeping well. Appetite good'. Three days later, clinical notes provide further details about his medical history:

> [Sergeant EF] has been very quiet and well-conducted and has been allowed out on pass accompanied by other companion patients. He seems rational in his conversation. He states the first fit he had was in 1904 in India; that he had two in 1905; had one in 1911; and one in 1915; and one last April. He describes a kind of sensory aura. States he knows when the fits are coming on as he gets a sensation of tightness about the chest for about four or five days prior to the fits. He states he began to lose power of the arm about three months ago. Sleeps and eats well.

Just 16 days after admission to the Richmond War Hospital, Sergeant EF was 'transferred to Belfast' War Hospital for further treatment.

Sergeant EF's clinical record provides a very clear description of epilepsy, with a prolonged, characteristic prodrome (period of time preceding a seizure, during which specific symptoms may herald the upcoming seizure),[48] although it is not clear from the records whether or not his epilepsy was due to an injury sustained while serving with the army at an earlier point. The observation that Sergeant EF was '*gradually* losing the power of his left arm' (italics added) is interesting, and it is noteworthy that Sergeant EF also demonstrated various other features of shellshock, including tremor, 'pain in his head', nervousness and insomnia. This complex relationship between epilepsy and the psychological effects of war is also apparent in the case of Private QR, a 22-year-old, single Roman Catholic private admitted to the Richmond War Hospital from King George V Hospital in early 1919.

Private QR was 'pale and delicate looking', with a 'scar of operation wound for appendicitis'. Mentally, 'he is a rather feeble-minded individual who states he suffers from epilepsy. He complains of headache and states any excitement upsets him'. Private QR had joined the army in 1914. He 'went to the Front in in September 1915 and was two years there. Was blown up and buried for two hours by shell fire and was sent home to England and was 6 months in hospital suffering from shell shock'. In 1917, he was discharged from the army on pension.

Private QR re-joined the army in 1918 and 'went to England' but 'got bad with epilepsy and was sent over to King George V Hospital, Dublin'. He was on leave from that hospital and 'got excited and fell down in a fit in the street and was carried into his own house and was brought back to King George V Hospital and was then sent here' (that is, to the Richmond War Hospital). 'He says he had two fits while in King George V Hospital, Dublin'.

On his first night at the War Hospital, Private QR 'remained quiet and slept well during the night'. One week after admission, clinical notes record that 'this man has much improved in his appearance. He is very quiet and well-conducted and gives no trouble. He has had no fits or attacks of excitement of any kind since he came here. Sleeps and eats well'.

Two weeks after admission, Private QR was still 'much improved physically, He has had no attacks of excitement since he came here. He is bright and cheerful and is allowed out on pass every day. Sleeps and eats well'. One month after admission, this improvement was sustained: 'He has had no fit since admission. He is bright and cheerful and gives no trouble. Sleeps and eats well'.

Six weeks after admission, clinical notes record that Private PQ remained 'improved in his appearance' and 'very quiet and well-conducted', but had '3 epileptic fits' in a single day, 'the first he has had since his admission'. Notwithstanding this temporary setback, clinical notes record that, after two months in the War Hospital, Private QR had had 'no further fits' and was 'quiet and well-conducted. Gives no trouble. Sleeps and eats well'. One month later, Private PQ was discharged from the War Hospital.

Clearly, Private PQ and Sergeant EF, like Private DE, presented to the Richmond War Hospital with a complex combination of physical and mental symptoms, all of which required care, quietude and medical attention. All three soldiers appear to have benefitted, to a significant extent, from their time at the Richmond War Hospital.

Similar cases, including cases of epilepsy and infectious diseases, were reported in other war hospitals, including Lord Derby War Hospital in Warrington, Lancashire,[49] which, like the Richmond, also recorded significant rates of recovery and discharge.[50] Epilepsy was also reported as a problem at Dykebar

War Hospital in Paisley[51] and Welsh Metropolitan War Hospital in Cardiff[52] where, as in Dykebar and Lord Derby War Hospitals, cases related to alcohol misuse also presented significant problems, accounting for 18 per cent of admissions at Dykebar[53] and 8 per cent at Lord Derby.[54] Problems with syphilis-related disorders were also reported at Dykebar[55] and Welsh Metropolitan War Hospital.[56]

The overall treatment paradigm at Lord Derby War Hospital appears to have been similar to that at the Richmond War Hospital, with particular emphasis on 'massage' and other 'specialised treatments', 'parole' from the hospital during convalescence, and 'employment on the farm and in the gardens of the hospital' for 'suitable cases'.[57] In addition, 'beds in the open air were provided for those to whom it was thought rest in bed would be beneficial'. At Metropolitan War Hospital, too, common treatments included bed rest, 'verandah treatment', dietary measures, baths, massage and parole, as well as provision of entertainments and work on the farm and in the gardens.[58]

## 'Excellent and Indeed Indispensable Work': Treatments at the Richmond War Hospital

Overall, the soldiers admitted to the Richmond War Hospital presented with characteristic features of shell shock and other psychological consequences of war, as well as other mental disorders and physical illnesses such as malaria and epilepsy. In 1925, the operation of the Richmond War Hospital was summarised by Lieutenant Colonel Dawson in the MPA's *Journal of Mental Science*, which described the energetic Dawson as follows: 'W.R. Dawson, O.B.E., M.D., Lt.-Col.; Chief Medical Officer, Ministry of Home Affairs, Northern Ireland; late H.M. Inspector of Asylums, Ireland; late Specialist in Nerve Diseases to the Troops in Ireland, etc.'[59]

In his paper, Dawson spoke highly of the Richmond War Hospital:

> Small as it was, this hospital, which was opened on June 16, 1916, did excellent and indeed indispensable work, thanks to the interest and support of Dr Donelan, the Resident Medical Superintendent, and of the staff concerned in its management, but especially, I feel justified in saying, of the late Dr MJ Forde, at that time Senior Assistant Medical Officer in charge of the male department, who devoted himself *con amore* to looking after these cases. From the date of opening until December 23, 1919, when this war hospital was closed, the records show 362 admissions, of whom about two-thirds were discharged to their friends or to ordinary military hospitals, two returned to duty, and only 31 were sent directly to civil asylums.

Useful as this institution proved, however, it was obviously too small to deal with all the mental cases occurring, and in October, 1916, a letter reached the Office of the Inspectors of Lunatics in Dublin from the Army Council, asking whether it would be possible to place at the disposal of the War Office a staffed and equipped asylum of about 500 beds, a number of asylums in Great Britain having been so handed over by transferring the inmates to other institutions. The difficulty in Ireland, however, lay in the already overcrowded condition of all the district asylums except three, none of which latter had any large number of vacant beds; and after full consideration the conclusion was reached that the only way in which the request of the Army Council could be acceded to was by removing the patients from the old Belfast Asylum in Grosvenor Road and disposing of them elsewhere.[60]

Dawson went on to provide a gripping account of Belfast War Hospital which admitted its first military patients on 15 May 1917 and remained in operation until 17 November 1919:

The total number of admissions to the hospital during its 2½ years of existence was 1,215, including 74 transferred from the Richmond War Hospital. Of these 18 returned to duty, 865 were discharged to the care of their friends, transferred to ordinary naval and military hospitals, or to institutions other than asylums (a few being otherwise disposed of), 21 died, and 306 were sent to civil mental hospitals or to other war hospitals. This gives a percentage of approximately 72 either recovered fully or sufficiently improved to be treated as ordinary sane individuals by the end of the period of existence of the hospital, which, together with a death-rate of 1.6 per cent, leaves only about 25 per cent not recovered or convalescent on removal from the institution.

It may also be added that a portion of what had formerly been the Resident Medical Superintendent's house was set apart for the treatment of officers, and in this department, the only Army provision in Ireland for mentally affected officers, a further 40 cases were treated.[61]

Overall, the statistics from Belfast are very comparable with those from the Richmond War Hospital, which was significantly smaller than its Belfast counterpart, and where RMS Donelan reported that more than half of the patients 'were successfully treated and enabled to return to their homes', although he also noted that, like in Belfast, treatment was not of benefit for one-quarter of the patients admitted.[62]

Interestingly, in his consideration of the Belfast War Hospital, Dawson pays remarkably little attention to the issue of treatment which, at the Richmond, included rest and quietude, various activities (outings, music and games), hot and cold baths, and a series of medicinal products, such as Fletcher's syrup of the hydrobromates, antipyrin and citrate of caffeine. Some of these treatment approaches were relatively new, but others, such as hydrotherapy, were consistent with long-established asylum practices,[63] as was the emphasis on observation. This was also consistent with the original intention of the military authorities who, in 1916, had sought accommodation at the Richmond to use as an 'observation hospital' for soldiers with nervous and mental troubles.[64]

In any case, the Richmond War Hospital closed its doors on 23 December 1919 having treated some 362 patients. While this was the end of operations at the Richmond War Hospital, however, the much larger Richmond District Asylum carried on for many more decades. The next chapter, Chapter Five, explores the story of the Richmond District Asylum after the closure of the War Hospital, with particular emphasis on the ways in which the establishment changed since the War Hospital closed. Conditions in the asylum during this period were, of course, of particular relevance to the minority of soldiers who were transferred there, or admitted there, during the 1920s, 1930s and beyond.

Finally, to conclude, Chapter Six examines the enduring legacy of the Richmond War Hospital, drawing together the story of the War Hospital in the context of the Irish asylum system and in the context of efforts to treat soldiers traumatised by the First World War in the various war hospitals throughout Ireland and Great Britain.

## Endnotes

[1] Howorth, P., 'The treatment of shell shock: Cognitive therapy before its time'. *Psychiatric Bulletin* 2000; 24: 225-7. The 1997 film *Regneration*, based on the novel of the same name by Pat Barker, provides superb demonstrations of various treatments for shell shock (Barker, 2014).

[2] This involved re-structuring the way the soldier viewed and interpreted past experiences; see: Rivers, W.H.R., 'An address on the repression of war experience'. *Lancet* 1918; i: 173-7.

[3] Bisson, J., Andrew, M., 'Psychological treatment of post-traumatic stress disorder (PTSD)'. *Cochrane Database of Systematic Reviews* 2007; 18: CD003388.

[4] War Office Committee of Enquiry into 'Shell-Shock'. *Report of the War Office Committee of Enquiry into 'Shell-Shock'.* London: HMSO, 1922.

[5] Ibid.

[6] Ibid, p. 158.

[7] Ibid, p. 192.

[8] Ibid.

[9] Reynolds, J., *Grangegorman: Psychiatric Care in Dublin since 1815.* Dublin: Institute of Public Administration in association with Eastern Health Board, 1992; pp. 218-9.

[10] See *The Irish Times* (11 October 1918) in relation to the treatment of shell shock at the Hermitage, Lucan, which reportedly achieved 'excellent results' in such cases; see also: 'A Grand Red Cross Fete & Horse-Jumping Competition' (*Irish Times*, 9 August 1917).

[11] 'Richmond War Hospital Admission and Discharge Book for Field Service (1916-1919)', National Archives of Ireland, Bishop Street, Dublin 8 (BR/PRIV 1223 Richmond War).

[12] Kelly, B.D., 'One hundred years ago: The Richmond Asylum, Dublin in 1907'. *Irish Journal of Psychological Medicine* 2007; 24: 108–14.

[13] Cherry, S., Munting, R., "Exercise is the thing?' Sport and the Asylum c1850-1950'. *International Journey of the History of Sport* 2005; 22: 42-58.

[14] Anonymous. Irish Division. *Journal of Mental Science* 1917; 63: 297-9.

[15] Bewley, T., *Madness to Mental Illness: A History of the Royal College of Psychiatrists.* London: Royal College of Psychiatrists, 2008; p. 10.

[16] Collins, A., 'Eleonora Fleury captured'. *British Journal of Psychiatry* 2013; 203: 5; p. 5; Bewley, T., *Madness to Mental Illness: A History of the Royal College of Psychiatrists.* London: Royal College of Psychiatrists, 2008; p. 27.

[17] Anonymous. Irish Division. *Journal of Mental Science* 1917; 63: 297-9; p. 298.

[18] Ibid.

[19] Ibid.

[20] Braslow, J.T., 'Punishment or therapy. Patients, doctors, and somatic remedies in the early twentieth century'. *Psychiatric Clinics of North America* 1994; 17: 493-513.

[21] War Office Committee of Enquiry into 'Shell-Shock', *Report of the War Office Committee of Enquiry into 'Shell-Shock'*; p. 192.

[22] Brune, K., 'The early history of non-opioid analgesics'. *Acute Pain* 1997; 1: 33-40.

[23] Burt, W.H., *Physiological Materia Medica (Containing All that is Known of the Physiological Action of Our Remedies Together with their Characteristic Indications and Pharmacology)* (Fifth Edition). Chicago: Gross & Delbridge Company, 1896; p. 321.

[24] Shorter, E., *A History of Psychiatry: From the Era of the Asylum to the Age of Prozac*. New York: John Wiley and Sons, 1997; pp. 201-202.

[25] *British Medical Journal*, 1 April 1882; p. 464. Reproduced from *British Medical Journal*, 1 April 1882 Volume 1; p. 464, with permission from BMJ Publishing Group Ltd.

[26] Walker, D., 'Modern nerves, nervous moderns: Notes on male neurasthenia'. In: Goldberg, S.L., Smith, F.B., *Australian Cultural History* (pp. 123-37). Cambridge: Cambridge University Press, 1988; p. 132.

[27] *Irish Times*, 6 December 1918.

[28] *Irish Times*, 22 May 1919.

[29] Anonymous. Irish Division. *Journal of Mental Science* 1917; 63: 297-9; p. 299.

[30] Kelly, B.D., 'Physical sciences and psychological medicine: The legacy of Prof John Dunne'. *Irish Journal of Psychological Medicine* 2005; 22: 67-72.

[31] Anonymous. Irish Division. *Journal of Mental Science* 1917; 63: 297-9; p. 299.

[32] Inspector of Lunatics (Ireland). *The Forty-Second Report (With Appendices) of the Inspector of Lunatics (Ireland)*. Dublin: Thom and Co./ Her Majesty's Stationery Office, 1893; p. 9.

[33] McCandless, P., 'Curative asylum, custodial hospital: The South Carolina Lunatic Asylum and State Hospital, 1828–1920'. In: Porter, R., Wright, D. (eds.) *The Confinement of the Insane: International Perspectives, 1800–1965* (pp. 173–92). Cambridge: Cambridge University Press, 2003.

[34] Inspectors of Lunatics (Ireland). *The Sixty-Fifth Annual Report (With Appendices) of the Inspectors of Lunatics (Ireland), Being for the Year Ending 31st December 1915.* Dublin: His Majesty's Stationery Office, 1917; p. xxiv.

[35] Inspectors of Lunatics (Ireland). *The Sixty-Seventh Annual Report (With Appendices) of the Inspectors of Lunatics (Ireland), Being for the Year Ending 31st December 1917.* Dublin: His Majesty's Stationery Office, 1919.

[36] Kelly, B.D., 'Tuberculosis in the nineteenth-century asylum: Clinical cases from the Central Criminal Lunatic Asylum, Dundrum, Dublin'. In: Prior P.M. (ed.) *Asylums, Mental Health Care and the Irish, 1800-2010* (pp. 205-20). Dublin and Portland, OR: Irish Academic Press, 2011.

[37] Inspectors of Lunatics (Ireland). *The Forty-Second Report (With Appendices) of the Inspectors of Lunatics (Ireland) 1892.* Dublin: Alexander Thom and Company (Limited) for Her Majesty's Stationery Office, 1893; p. 7.

[38] Finnane, P., *Insanity and the Insane in Post-Famine Ireland.* London: Croom Helm, 1981; p. 137.

[39] Jones, G., 'The Campaign Against Tuberculosis in Ireland, 1899-1914'. In: Malcolm, E., Jones, G. (eds.) *Medicine, Disease and the State in Ireland, 1650-1940* (pp. 158-76). Cork: Cork University Press, 1999.

[40] McCandless, *The Confinement of the Insane.*

[41] Reynolds, *Grangegorman*; Kelly, B.D., 'One hundred years ago: The Richmond Asylum, Dublin in 1907'. *Irish Journal of Psychological Medicine* 2007; 24: 108–14.

[42] Norman, C.J., *Richmond Asylum Joint Committee Minutes.* Dublin: Richmond Asylum, 1907; p. 540.

[43] Hotchkis, R.D., 'Renfrew District Asylum as a war hospital for mental invalids: Some contrasts in administration with an analysis of cases admitted during the first year'. *Journal of Mental Science* 1917; 63: 238-49; p. 247.

[44] Richardson, N.A., *Coward if I Return, A Hero if I Fall: Stories of Irishmen in World War I.* Dublin: The O'Brien Press, 2010; pp. 154, 203, 243, 316. For further stories of Irish soldiers in the First World War, see: Dungan, M., *They Shall Grow Not Old: Irish Soldiers and the Great War.* Dublin: Four Courts Press Limited, 1997.

[45] Barton White, E., 'Abstract of a report on the mental division of the Welsh Metropolitan War Hospital, Whitchurch, Cardiff, September, 1917–September, 1919'. *Journal of Mental Science* 1920; 66: 438-49; p. 440.

[46] Anonymous. Irish Division. *Journal of Mental Science* 1917; 63: 297-9; p. 298.

[47] Atenstaedt, R.L., 'Trench fever: The British medical response in the Great War'. *Journal of the Royal Society of Medicine* 2006; 99: 564–8.

[48] Clarke, C.R.A., 'Neurological diseases and diseases of voluntary muscle'. In: Kumar, P., Clark, M. (eds), *Clinical Medicine* (pp. 871-955). London: Ballière Tindall, 1994; pp. 912-3.

[49] Henderson, D.K., 'War psychoses: An analysis of 202 cases of mental disorder occurring in home troops'. *Journal of Mental Science* 1918; 64: 165-89; p. 185.

[50] Eager, R., 'A record of admissions to the mental section of the Lord Derby War Hospital, Warrington, from June 17th, 1916 to June 16th, 1917'. *Journal of Mental Science* 1918; 64: 272-96; pp. 274, 294. See also: Henderson, D.K., 'War psychoses: An analysis of 202 cases of mental disorder occurring in home troops'. *Journal of Mental Science* 1918; 64: 165-89; p. 166.

[51] Hotchkis, R.D., 'Renfrew District Asylum as a war hospital for mental invalids: Some contrasts in administration with an analysis of cases admitted during the first year'. *Journal of Mental Science* 1917; 63: 238-49; p. 248.

[52] Barton White, E., 'Abstract of a report on the mental division of the Welsh Metropolitan War Hospital, Whitchurch, Cardiff, September, 1917–September, 1919'. *Journal of Mental Science* 1920; 66: 438-49; p. 444.

[53] Hotchkis, R.D., 'Renfrew District Asylum as a war hospital for mental invalids: Some contrasts in administration with an analysis of cases admitted during the first year'. *Journal of Mental Science* 1917; 63: 238-49; p. 244.

[54] Henderson, D.K., 'War psychoses: An analysis of 202 cases of mental disorder occurring in home troops'. *Journal of Mental Science* 1918; 64: 165-89; p. 180. See also: Eager, R., 'A record of admissions to the mental section of the Lord Derby War Hospital, Warrington, from June 17th, 1916 to June 16th, 1917'. *Journal of Mental Science* 1918; 64: 272-96; p. 274.

[55] Hotchkis, R.D., 'Renfrew District Asylum as a war hospital for mental invalids: Some contrasts in administration with an analysis of cases admitted during the first year'. *Journal of Mental Science* 1917; 63: 238-49; p. 247.

[56] Barton White, E., 'Abstract of a report on the mental division of the Welsh Metropolitan War Hospital, Whitchurch, Cardiff, September, 1917–September, 1919'. *Journal of Mental Science* 1920; 66: 438-49; p. 444.

[57] Eager, R., 'A record of admissions to the mental section of the Lord Derby War Hospital, Warrington, from June 17th, 1916 to June 16th, 1917'. *Journal of Mental Science* 1918; 64: 272-96; pp. 294-5.

[58] Barton White, E., 'Abstract of a report on the mental division of the Welsh Metropolitan War Hospital, Whitchurch, Cardiff, September, 1917–September, 1919'. *Journal of Mental Science* 1920; 66: 438-49; p. 445.

[59] Dawson, W.R., 'The work of the Belfast War Hospital (1917-1919)'. *Journal of Mental Science* 1925; 71: 219-24; p. 219.

[60] Ibid, pp. 219-20.

[61] Ibid, pp. 220-21. See also: 'Sir Edward Carson in Belfast', *Irish Times*, 23 July 1917.

[62] Quoted in: Reynolds, *Grangegorman*, p. 219.

[63] Braslow, J.T., 'Punishment or therapy. Patients, doctors, and somatic remedies in the early twentieth century'. *Psychiatric Clinics of North America* 1994; 17: 493-513.

[64] Reynolds, *Grangegorman*; p. 217.

# 5

## The Richmond Asylum after the War Hospital (1919– )

The Richmond War Hospital closed on 23 December 1919. Over the three-and-a-half years it was in operation, 362 patients had been admitted and more than half of these 'were successfully treated and enabled to return to their homes without the blemish of having been certified insane', according to RMS Donelan.[1]

At that time, 'being certified insane' was indeed seen as a 'blemish', not least owing to the grim reputation of Ireland's asylums and the dark associations the public drew between the asylums, mental illness and those affected it.

The Richmond War Hospital was, in many ways, an exception to that rather gloomy picture: patients in the War Hospital were not certified as 'insane'; the accommodation and treatments at the War Hospital were relatively benign;[2] and there was a reportedly high rate of therapeutic success.[3] At the monthly meeting of the Joint Committee of Management of the Richmond District Lunatic Asylum in February 1920, two months after the Richmond War Hospital closed, the formal gratitude of the War Office for the work of the War Hospital was noted:

A letter was read from the Secretary of the War Office stating that, in connection with the closing down of the

Richmond War Hospital, Dublin, he was commanded by the Army Council to express their thanks to the Joint Committee of the Richmond District Asylum, Dublin, for their generosity and for their great efforts, upon which from June 1916, till December last this hospital had been dependent. The Council deeply appreciated the kind and patriotic action which had rendered possible the provision and maintenance of so valuable an addition to the medical resources of the Army as the Richmond War Hospital had proved itself to be. Further, he requested that the Joint Committee would be good enough to convey to the staff of the hospital the thanks of the Army Council for the whole-hearted attention and devotion which they had given to the patients who had been under their care.[4]

The closure of both the Richmond and Belfast War Hospitals in 1919[5] did, however, present challenges to the broader Irish asylum system, as a review of the *69th Annual Report of the Inspectors of Lunatics (Ireland) for the year 1919* published in the *Journal of Mental Science* in 1921 noted:

As would have been expected, the reduction in numbers which had been noted in the immediately preceding years, and which had been attributed to the well-known effects of a prolonged war upon the insane population, has not been fully maintained with the conclusion of the European War. Whereas the reduction during the year 1918 amounted to over 1,000 patients, on this occasion it amounts to but 290, the actual figures being 22,578, which give a proportion of 515 insane persons per 100,000 of the estimated population.

The number of admissions, at 3,956 patients, has risen by 463. The cause of this increase is to be discerned in the fact that the Belfast and Richmond War Hospitals were closed towards the end of the period under review, thus terminating a most useful chapter in the career of the parent institutions under whose care these excellent hospitals had been maintained. The patients who were not considered fit to be discharged have been transferred to the civil asylums under the kindly designation of 'service patients'.[6]

Following the closure of the Richmond War Hospital in 1919, Donelan suggested the vacated building might be used for private patients who would be able to pay something towards the cost of their maintenance.[7] While it is clear that this interesting suggestion did not progress any further, it is still worth exploring whether or not, after the closure of the Richmond War Hospital, any of its other interesting and often progressive initiatives, especially its relatively benign approach to treatment, were maintained in the Richmond District Asylum and throughout Ireland's asylum system in general.

Conditions in the Irish asylums during the first part of the twentieth century are, of course, of particular relevance to the minority of soldiers who were not discharged home or back to service from the Richmond War Hospital but transferred instead to regular asylums. Dawson, in his 1925 paper in the *Journal of Mental Science*, noted that, of the 362 patients treated at the Richmond War Hospital, 'about two-thirds were discharged to their friends or to ordinary military hospitals, two returned to duty [0.6 per cent], and only 31 were sent directly to civil asylums'.[8] Neil Richardson, in his fascinating, invaluable collection of 'stories of Irishmen in World War I', titled *A Coward if I Return, A Hero if I Fall*, tells the story of Bill Hand, an Irishman who served at Gallipoli and Ypres, where he experienced shell fire and witnessed violent deaths at close range.[9] Mr Hand developed shell shock after his return home and was eventually placed in a psychiatric institution; his children told his grandchildren that he had died whereas, in fact, he lived until 1963, at which point he died alone.

What was life like for this minority of Irish soldiers who ended up in asylums during the first half of the twentieth century? Did the relatively enlightened approach of the Richmond War Hospital persist? What, if anything, was the enduring legacy of the War Hospital for the Richmond District Asylum in particular? Did the War Hospital simply disappear without trace, or did it have a lasting impact on the institution and beyond?

## Therapeutic Enthusiasm at the Richmond District Asylum in the 1900s

The more positive approach to treatment seen in the Richmond War Hospital was somewhat curtailed in most Irish asylums throughout the 1920s by persistent overcrowding and various institutional problems. In 1924, Edward Boyd Barrett, SJ MA, drew particular attention to the lack of effective treatment in the asylums, in an article in *Studies*, an influential 'Irish Quarterly Review':

> Thanks to this indifference of the public, our asylums are in a bad way. They are over-crowded. They are both understaffed and inefficiently staffed. Curable and incurable cases are herded together. There is practically no treatment. The percentage of cures remains at a very low figure. Public money is wasted. The asylums are unsuited for their purpose in almost every respect.[10]

Therapeutic enthusiasm was, however, soon to the fore again in the 1930s, especially following the appointment of a new RMS at the Richmond, Dr John Dunne. Dunne 'had made a name for himself when, as an assistant medical officer, he had introduced malarial treatment for patients suffering from general paralysis of the insane' (a form of advanced syphilis affecting the brain).[11]

Malarial therapy was based on the clinical observation that certain individuals with mental disorder improved when they got an infection, so doctors developed a 'malarial fever' cure which involved inoculating patients with malaria.[12] The chief proponent of this approach, Dr Julius Wagner-Jauregg (1857–1940), won a Nobel Prize for this work in 1927, although the 'fever cure' did not prove of lasting worth and was later abandoned owing to limited efficacy, severe adverse effects and high cost.[13]

At Grangegorman Mental Hospital (as the Richmond was re-named under the Local Government Act 1925), Dunne's enthusiasms extended well beyond novel physical therapies such as malarial therapy, however, as he introduced many pragmatic and positive changes to the vast establishment, including:

- Removal of benches that were used to hem in challenging patients;
- Employment of extra attendants to give patients more liberty;
- Replacement of old box beds with cast iron bedsteads;
- Establishment of a medical library to keep staff in touch with scientific developments; and,
- Efforts to establish a separate unit for the disturbed elderly and a separate ward for children.[14]

Many of these changes had been prefigured by the relatively enlightened approach of the Richmond War Hospital two decades earlier. Dunne, however, also retained his interest in novel treatments for mental disorder and, as the twentieth century progressed, various new physical treatments were introduced at Grangegorman, including insulin coma therapy, frontal lobotomy (leucotomy) and electroconvulsive therapy (ECT). Dunne went on to serve as president of the MPA in 1955, when the organisation held its annual meeting in Dublin.[15]

In his 1950 *Survey of modern physical methods of treatment for mental illness carried out in Grangegorman Mental Hospital*, Dunne struck a generally optimistic note about the potential of novel physical treatments for mental disorder at Grangegorman:

> These physical methods are mainly empirical and may be described under three headings – convulsive treatment, insulin coma treatment and psycho-surgery. While the *modus operandi* of these treatments has not been satisfactorily explained there can be no doubt that they represent a revolution in the medical approach to mental illness and that it is only a matter of time until the aetiology of mental disease is sufficiently understood to allow treatment on a more scientific and rational basis.[16]

Insulin therapy had been introduced by Manfred Sakel (1900–57), an Austrian psychiatrist and neurophysiologist, in the early 1930s and initially involved administering insulin to individuals with mental disorder in order to increase weight and inhibit excitement.[17] Sakel noted, however, that the unintentional comas occasionally induced by insulin appeared to produce remission in schizophrenia. As a result, inducing coma was soon regarded as the key therapeutic mechanism of insulin.[18]

In July 1938, Dunne introduced insulin coma therapy at Grangegorman.[19] Dunne reported that the first patient to receive the treatment, a twenty-five-year-old woman, recovered sufficiently to return home. In 1940, he reported that a significant proportion of patients continued to recover and, in 1950, that 405 out of 605 patients with schizophrenia (67 per cent) recovered.[20] There were two fatalities, one from acute pancreatitis and one from acute pulmonary oedema. Dunne concluded that 'insulin has a certain specificity for schizophrenia', unlike ECT which, he concluded, was indicated for the 'affective disorders

[for example, depression] and neuroses [for example, anxiety]'
(see below).[21]

Insulin coma therapy was not available during the First
World War and so was not used at the Richmond War Hospital,
but it was used elsewhere on soldiers during the Second World
War.[22] Insulin coma was, in fact, used quite widely around the
world during the 1940s and 1950s, although it was increasingly
recognised that the risks and adverse effects were such that it
could only be performed in fully equipped centres with specialised staff.[23] While there were some suggestions that insulin therapy may be useful in depression, it was used chiefly in
schizophrenia.[24] Insulin therapy went into decline in the early
1960s owing to the emergence of safer and more effective treatments (chiefly anti-psychotic medication),[25] but, even by 1964,
it has not disappeared entirely.[26]

Frontal lobotomy (leucotomy), a form of brain surgery, was
another form of physical treatment used at Grangegorman and
elsewhere. While brain surgery has a very long history in medicine, frontal lobotomy or leucotomy (which involves surgery on
the frontal part of the brain), was introduced in 1935 by Dr An-
tónio Egas Moniz (1874–1955), a Portuguese neurologist who
shared a Nobel Prize for his work in 1949.[27] The practice was
adopted enthusiastically in the United States by Dr Walter Free-
man (1895–1972) who performed up to 3,500 lobotomies over
the course of his career.[28]

According to some texts, lobotomy reduced feelings of anxiety and introspection, as well as emotional tension and catatonia (severe mental disorder).[29] As a result, patients appeared to
become more placid and tranquil,[30] with significant reductions
in symptom expression.[31]

Again, while there is no evidence that psycho-surgery was
used at the Richmond War Hospital during the First World

War, it was used elsewhere among soldiers in the Second World War.[32] At Grangegorman, leucotomy was introduced in April 1946 when A.A. McConnell was engaged to perform the procedure at the nearby Richmond Hospital.[33] Dunne was keenly aware of 'the serious nature of the operation' and so the 'cases selected were advanced schizophrenics, who had failed to improve with prolonged courses of insulin and ECT and who on account of their impulsive, negativistic, suicidal or homicidal tendencies were a source of constant strain and worry and upset to the nursing staff and a danger to the other patients and to themselves'.[34]

By June 1947, 23 leucotomies had been performed on patients resident in Grengegorman, with mixed results.[35] In 1950, Dunne reported more extensive and detailed outcome data:

> Out of a total of 63 schizophrenic patients, for whom it could be said there was practically no hope of even amelioration of symptoms, 19 recovered sufficiently to be discharged from hospital; 19 improved considerably in behaviour; 18 showed no change and 4 showed marked disimprovement; 3 died. It must be admitted that the majority of these schizophrenics who were discharged, although showing a vast improvement generally in their mental states and hailed by their relatives as perfect recoveries, would not be regarded by the scientific eye as perfectly integrated personalities.[36]

In 1952, Dr David Stafford-Clark, a leading psychiatrist, wrote at length about the controversial operation ('a remarkable combination of brilliance and crudity'), advising great care, but still concluding that it had a role in certain cases.[37] Despite some lingering enthusiasm for the operation, leucotomy went into decline during the 1950s, owing to its adverse effects and lack of efficacy, as well as the arrival of alternative, safer treatments. As a result, the standard operation became less popular and leucotomies were more frequently of a less traumatic variety.[38]

Overall, from today's perspective, the story of leucotomy is one of therapeutic enthusiasm that went unchecked for too long.[39] This enthusiasm found its roots in a deep desire to alleviate mental suffering and discharge people from large, unsuitable mental hospitals, but, from today's perspective, the resultant enthusiasm was taken to an unacceptable extreme, with the result that the procedure itself was used too widely and for too long, sometimes (although not always) with tragic results.[40]

## Integrating Treatments, Old and New

It is interesting to compare the story of leucotomy with that of ECT, another treatment which became popular in the mid-1900s, and was used at Grangegorman from the 1940s onwards. ECT involves the use of electricity, applied across the brain, to produce epileptic-type seizures (convulsions or fits) and was initially based on the idea that seizures were therapeutic in individuals with mental disorder.[41] On this basis, programmes of convulsive therapy were introduced by Dr Ladislas Joseph Meduna (1896–1964), a Hungarian neurologist who would, in 1938, go on to develop *electro*convulsive therapy, with Dr Ugo Cerletti (1877–1963), an Italian neurologist at the Rome University Psychiatric Clinic.[42]

In the early years, seizures were induced using chemicals rather than electricity. Cardiazol was the trade-name of pentamethylenetetrazol, a camphor-like compound, initially used by Meduna for convulsive treatment of schizophrenia.[43] In 1935, Meduna reported positive results in ten out of the first 26 of his patients to receive Cardiazol treatment.[44] As a result, convulsive treatment soon spread to psychiatric centres throughout Europe and beyond. The first recorded use of Cardiazol in England appears to have been at Moorcroft House, a private institution in Middlesex, in 1937. As the 1930s progressed, Cardiazol treatment became the most widely used physical treatment in public mental hospitals in Great Britain.[45] The first recorded use of Cardiazol in Ireland was at St Brigid's Hospital, Ballinasloe in 1939.[46]

As was the case with insulin coma therapy and psycho-surgery, there is no evidence that electricity or convulsive therapy were used at the Richmond War Hospital, but there is evidence of the use of electricity as part of treatment elsewhere during the First World War[47] and the use of convulsive therapy elsewhere for soldiers in the Second World War too.[48]

Convulsive therapy, using electricity rather than Cardiazol to produce seizures, was introduced at Grangegorman in April 1942.[49] Eight years later, Dunne presented the results of 765 patients who received ECT, outlining the proportion of these who had 'recovered' following the procedure, by which he meant 'patients in whom symptoms disappeared and who on discharge maintained their recovery and succeeded in adjusting themselves to their environment'.[50] Among the patients with 'involutional melancholia' (that is, depression; 327 patients), 64 per cent recovered; among those with 'manic depressive' illness (153 patients), 59 per cent recovered; and among those with schizophrenia (191 patients), only 12 per cent recovered. Accordingly, Dunne concluded that 'ECT should only be given for affective states, namely, prolonged manic-depressive phases, involutional mental states and neuroses where anxiety is a prominent feature and which have not yielded to the full use of psycho-somatic therapy'.

Dunne's writings about ECT provide an excellent example of how his interest in physical methods of treatment was coupled with a real desire to examine their outcomes and determine their precise roles. Dunne not only presented systematic examinations of outcomes and indications for specific treatments, but also advised against indiscriminate use of *any* treatments:

> It is not inopportune at this stage to issue a word of warning with regard to the danger of placing too much reliance on empirical methods. Experience has shown that any particular syndrome may be brought about by bodily or psychological disorder, successful treatment of which can abort the consequent and more serious mental symptoms. A painstaking and exhausting investigation should always be carried out before resorting to empirical methods... The case with which shock treatment can be given and the dramatic results that follow in properly selected cases have led to a tendency of indiscriminate use of empirical methods on a hit or miss basis, often with detrimental effects, thus perhaps making irreversible conditions which would probably have responded to other methods of treatment.[51]

Dunne's point about administering specific treatments only to 'properly selected cases' has strong echoes of the relatively benign treatment approach of the Richmond War Hospital,[52] and also remains relevant today, especially in relation to ECT. In 2010, the National Institute for Clinical Excellence in the United Kingdom examined the scientific evidence for ECT and now recommends that ECT for 'rapid and short-term improvement of severe symptoms after an adequate trial of other treatment options has proven ineffective and/or when the condition is con-sidered to be potentially life-threatening, in individuals with, se-vere depressive illness, catatonia, or a prolonged or severe manic episode.'[53] As Dunne pointed out some 60 years earlier, careful selection of patients for ECT remains imperative.

All of these treatments (insulin coma therapy, leucotomy, ECT) post-dated the Richmond War Hospital, where the treat-ment paradigms related back to the 'moral management' of the 1800s and psychotherapeutic approaches of the early 1900s, rather than the physical therapies that defined mental hospital care later in the 1900s. Inevitably the roles of these much-heralded physical therapies continued to evolve as the 1900s progressed, as indications for some (for example, ECT) were refined and others (for example, insulin coma therapy) dropped out of use entirely, in the broader context of systematic reform of Ireland's mental health system from the mid-1900s onwards.

Overall, the movement away from the key principles of 'moral management' in the early 1900s likely contributed, in significant part, to the continued and intensified problems experienced in the Irish psychiatric institutions in the mid-twentieth century, and suboptimal patient outcomes. Ironically, the overall direction of reform in the late twentieth century was *away* from the interventionist approaches of the 1930s, 1940s and 1950s, and back towards the paradigm reflected in the Richmond War Hospital, defined by a bio-psycho-social approach to care, involving gainful occupation as much as medicinal remedies, increasing focus on the quality of patient experience during the recovery process and, as a result, enhancing patient outcomes.[54]

## The Beginning of the End: Grangegorman in the 1950s and 1960s

The effects of the Second World War on Grangegorman were significantly less than the effects of the First World War, chiefly owing to Ireland's increasing disconnection from Great Britain: the Irish Free State had been founded in 1922 and a new Constitution, *Bunreacht na hÉireann*, naming the state Ireland (Éire), came into effect in 1937, two years prior to the Second World War. In contrast with the establishment of the Richmond War Hospital during the First World War, the chief effect of the Second World War was to delay building works at Grangegorman.[55]

At national level, reform of Ireland's mental health system took a significant step forward in the 1940s with the introduc-

tion of the Mental Treatment Act 1945, which clearly established a voluntary admission status and increased medical involvement in committal.[56] Notwithstanding this long-overdue
development, the number of psychiatric inpatients continued
to rise: by 1961, one in every 70 Irish people above the age of 24
was in a psychiatric hospital.[57] This was a real disappointment:
one of the key innovations of the Richmond War Hospital had
been that patients did not have to be certified as 'insane' in order to be admitted, but when a similar, voluntary patient status
was introduced more broadly in 1945, it did not bring about the
sweeping transformation of the asylum system that was both
needed and desired.

During this time, St Brendan's Hospital (as Grangegorman
was known since 1958) remained to the forefront of psychiatric
care but its long-standing problems with overcrowding persisted well into the 1950s and 1960s. In 1965, Dunne retired
as RMS, having brought about many changes at the hospital
during his tenure there.[58] As Reynolds points out, Dunne had
'inherited a monolithic institution where the patients received
little more than custodial care.'[59] Dunne had insisted that at least
some of the patients 'could improve under proper treatment
and were entitled to the same medical and scientific expertise
as was available to the physically ill.' In addition, Dunne had
brought unprecedented rigour to his examination of the outcome of common therapies[60] and documented the increasing
role of outpatient care in the evolution of Irish mental health
services, on a voluntary as opposed to involuntary basis.[61]

Following Dunne's retirement in 1965, Dr Ivor Browne,
then working at St Loman's Hospital in Palmerstown, was appointed Chief Psychiatrist in his place. Browne had already,
with Dr Dermot Walsh, written a plan for the development of
mental health services in Dublin, based on dividing the city and

county into districts and creating 'psychiatric teams...to serve each district and related not to a hospital but to the population of the area served.'[62] In the event, Browne was appointed to the position of Chief Psychiatrist and, on arrival at St Brendan's Hospital in 1965, quickly realized there was much work to be done to modernise and improve the situation at the hospital:

> I was faced with the onerous task of trying to initiate some change or movement in an antiquated, appallingly overcrowded, chaotic situation. The morale among the patients and staff could hardly have been lower. The hopelessly understaffed medical personnel were almost as institutionalized as the patients. I felt that some radical initiative that would grasp the attention of the public, and of the patients and staff of the hospital, was necessary if a perception that real change was beginning was to take hold.[63]

Browne set about the task with enthusiasm, making changes to structure and staffing at the hospital, as well as building up community mental health facilities around the city. Like Dunne, Browne also became professor of psychiatry at University College Dublin, giving him both 'teaching responsibilities and a heavy clinical and administrative commitment.'[64] Despite these considerable duties, Browne continued with efforts to modernise St Brendan's at a time of considerable change and challenge in psychiatric practice both in Ireland and abroad.

One of the most notable developments in psychiatry immediately prior to this period was the discovery and introduction of antipsychotic medication. The most significant of these medications, chlorpromazine, came to prominence in the 1950s when Jean Delay and Pierre Deniker, two Paris psychiatrists, published clinical data indicating its usefulness for the treatment of psychosis, thus introducing the first effective medication for schizophrenia.[65] Initially investigated as an anaesthetic, the effectiveness of chlorpromazine as an anti-psychotic medication soon had far-reaching effects, especially in reducing the use of physical restraints in psychiatric hospitals.[66]

Chlorpromazine was classed as a 'major tranquilizer'[67] and appeared to reduce the intensity of emotional states without substantial reductions of intellectual functions.[68] As such, it might, perhaps, have been useful for certain patients at the Richmond War Hospital, had it been available. Some 1960s commentators were even more enthusiastic about chlorpromazine, however, and saw it and related medications (known as 'phenothiazines') as more than simply tranquilizers and as potentially reversing the very pathology of schizophrenia.[69]

While these new medications undoubtedly helped alleviate severe mental disorder for many patients at St Brendan's and elsewhere, dismantling institutional structures such as St Brendan's was to require much more than just medication. Societal change and media pressure, especially in the late 1960s, made vital contributions to the eventual decline in Irish inpatient numbers. In October 1968, the *Irish Times* published an influential series of articles by Michael Viney highlighting the broad range of problems related to mental health care in Ireland generally and, in particular, the disproportionately large number of individuals still resident in Irish psychiatric hospitals:[70]

> In no other country in Europe – nor, probably, in the world – did so large a fraction of the nation's population find themselves in such surroundings. Comparatively few of these 19,656 people spoke to a doctor yesterday or are likely to speak to one today. And in a more prosperous and progressive society, one third of them (at a rough but not a reckless guess) would have left hospital years ago or would never have been admitted.
>
> They may long since have recovered from the illness which brought them into hospital. But they have lost their place in

the world outside: no home, no friends, no job. If they have an illness now, it is the one called 'institutional neurosis': a steady sapping of interest and initiative, an ever-growing dependence on the security, authority and routine of mental hospital life.[71]

At St Brendan's, change was clearly challenging throughout the 1960s, but there were definite signs of progress. Programmes were introduced to activate and engage chronic patients, many of whom were intellectually disabled rather than mentally ill.[72] Patients were encouraged to join therapeutic groups with the aim of improving skills for community living and social engagement. Ben Bono, a Dublin variety artist, was employed as recreation officer. These measures, which involved patients and staff alike, gave added impetus to the move away from the old asylum model of care and towards the kind of services that would later be made explicit in a new national mental health policy, *Planning for the Future*.[73] These measures were also highly reminiscent of the involvement of voluntary organisations, drama groups and choirs at the Richmond War Hospital, some 50 years earlier:[74] *plus ça change, plus c'est la même chose.*

## Moving to the Community: *Planning for the Future* and *A Vision for Change*

Throughout the 1970s, the reform process gathered pace at St Brendan's. One of the key reforms during Browne's time at the hospital was the establishment of a new 'assessment unit', designed to reduce the admission rate while also providing appropriate care through psychiatric teams covering each geographical catchment area:

Once the assessment unit was opened in St Brendan's, all patients who presented at the hospital were held overnight until next morning when they were either discharged or passed onto their appropriate sector service. By this means the catchment areas were now forced to undertake work for which they were established in the first place.

For the ten years preceding the establishment of the assessment unit in April 1979, the admission rate to St Brendan's had been running at over 2,000 patients per year. In 1978 the number of direct admission to the hospital was 2,676. By 1980, one year later, this figure had dropped to 1,558. Needless to say, this made a significant difference to overcrowding in the hospital and allowed breathing space to carry out further reorganisation within the institution.[75]

Much of this reform programme depended on the establishment of community mental health teams to provide effective alternatives to hospital admission. Other reforms included the establishment of specialist services for the homeless ('under the direction of Dr Joe Fernandez') and for 'those suffering from chronic alcoholism' (St Dymphna's), as well as closure of the 'Lower House', the oldest part of the hospital.[76]

Many of these moves were to be echoed and expanded in 1984 when a new national mental health policy, *Planning for the Future*, finally, formally paved the way for a definitive shift to community care.[77] *Planning for the Future* was an important document which directed that psychiatric services should be comprehensive and community-oriented, aimed at delivering care that is continuous, coordinated and multi-disciplinary. The population was divided into geographical sectors, each comprising 25,000 to 30,000 individuals. Care was to be delivered by consultant-led multi-disciplinary teams in each sector. The policy recommended that a dedicated crisis team be developed in each sector and additional specialized services be developed to cover more than one sector. Day hospitals were directed to provide intensive treatment equivalent to that available in inpatient settings for acutely ill patients.

With regard to specialised treatments, the policy addressed a number of specific areas, including liaison psychiatry services, rehabilitation programmes, the psychiatry of learning disability, services for the elderly, forensic psychiatry and mental health research. Treatment for children with mental health problems was also covered, as the authors recommended the establishment of one child guidance team per 200,000 population, and development of community-based interventions for alcohol-related problems, aimed at prevention rather than treatment.[78]

Almost twenty years after the publication of *Planning for the Future*, the Mental Health Commission, in its 2002 *Annual Report*, pointed out that the principles outlined in *Planning For The Future* were still relevant to psychiatric care in Ireland, and that while all of its recommendations had not yet been implemented, *Planning For The Future* had succeeded in bringing significant improvements to Irish psychiatric services, particularly in relation to de-institutionalisation.[79] Nonetheless, considerable challenges remained, relating to both specific service areas, such as services for the elderly,[80] and the continued use of unsuitable facilities for inpatient care.[81]

The Inspector of Mental Hospitals drew particular attention to St Brendan's, and reported ongoing challenges transitioning the hospital from its long history as a large inpatient facility to becoming part of a community-oriented service:

> Many of the patients in the current units [within St Brendan's], as well as most of those in the admission units and in the Willows required community placements and intensive rehabilitation. For this, more accommodation was required in the community and a specialised rehabilitation unit and team for St Brendan's Hospital. While a second consultant post in the psychiatry of the homeless had been created, the post had not been filled: it was clear that a reorientation towards an innovative,

well-resourced service for the homeless was needed, building on the current provision, which while centralised in its community aspects, on the streets and working in close harmony with related agencies in this field, would be decentralised in its acute in-patient requirements.[82]

At national level, the Inspector noted that 'despite the considerable progress that has been accomplished in replacing or improving inpatient premises, there were still some locations that were unacceptable for care and treatment of patients because of seriously unsatisfactory conditions.'[83] The Inspector went on to list specific 'inpatient black-spots' around the country and included 'the entire St Brendan's Hospital' second on his list (after 'most of the Central Mental Hospital').

This was a far cry from the progressive approach of the Richmond War Hospital almost a century earlier. Happily, the decade following the Inspector's 2003 report duly saw considerable change in the organisation of services both at St Brendan's and nationally, underpinned by the publication of a new national mental policy in 2006, titled *A Vision for Change*.[84] The new policy outlined a framework for promoting positive mental health in all sectors of the community and providing accessible specialist services for individuals with mental disorder.

In essence, the 2006 policy re-affirmed many of the principles outlined in *Planning for the Future* but added a renewed emphasis on implementation and an overall approach remarkably similar to that in evidence at the Richmond War Hospital at the start of the 1900s.[85] The 2006 policy provided detailed projections of the inpatient and outpatient resources needed for community-oriented mental health services, and presented specific suggestions on resourcing:

In the process of auditing the physical resources available to mental health services, special attention should be given to the old mental hospitals that still exist in parts of the country. Many of the human resources required for the model of service provision detailed in this report are currently still attached to mental hospitals. In order to free up these resources and to provide community-based, multidisciplinary team-delivered mental health care for all, existing mental hospitals will be required to close.[86]

This strong emphasis on closure of old hospitals as a pre-requisite for developing community-based treatment added greatly to the impetus to re-configure mental services, such as that at St Brendan's, so as to provide community-based mental health care, backed up by modern inpatient facilities when needed. Following a dedicated and extensive process of change and reform at St Brendan's and the associated services, in 2013, after two centuries of mental health care on the site, the old asylum buildings at St Brendan's were finally and fully closed to admissions, replaced by modern, community-based mental health services.[87]

Thus, after 200 eventful years of mental health care on the site, the era of the large asylum at Grangegorman finally came to an end. The old system was replaced by a network of community facilities operated by multi-disciplinary mental health teams, in accordance with both *Planning for the Future* (1984) and *A Vision for Change* (2006). In addition, the Phoenix Care Centre, on the North Circular Road, now provides a regional psychiatric intensive care service for individuals with acute episodes of major mental illnesses such as schizophrenia and bipolar affective disorder who cannot have their needs adequately met elsewhere. It provides specialist multidisciplinary treatment within a setting of low therapeutic security such that people may return to local psychiatric units to complete their treatment and thereafter be discharged home.

Much of the rest of the old Grangegorman campus is now occupied by Dublin Institute of Technology (DIT), one of Ireland's largest third-level institutions. DIT offers a broad range of under-graduate and post-graduate programmes in a wide range of disciplines, and has well-developed access and community service programmes, aiming to promote civic engagement and broaden participation in education.

As a result, some two centuries after the Richmond was established as a national leader in mental health care, a century-and-a-half after Lalor made the Richmond schools the envy of the world, and almost a century after the Richmond War Hospital opened its doors, Grangegorman had again moved its twin commitments, to mental health care and accessible education, forward into a new and exciting era. The final conclusions from the stories of the Richmond Asylum in general, and the Richmond War Hospital in particular, are considered next, in the final chapter of this complicated, involving and evolving story.

### Endnotes

[1] Reynolds, J., *Grangegorman: Psychiatric Care in Dublin since 1815*. Dublin: Institute of Public Administration in association with Eastern Health Board, 1992; p. 219.

[2] Anonymous. Irish Division. *Journal of Mental Science* 1917; 63: 297-9; Reynolds, Grangegorman; pp. 218-9.

[3] Dawson, W.R., 'The work of the Belfast War Hospital'. *Journal of Mental Science* 1925; 71: 219-24; pp. 219-20.

[4] *Irish Times*, 20 February 1920.

[5] Dawson, W.R., 'The work of the Belfast War Hospital (1917-1919)'. *Journal of Mental Science* 1925; 71: 219-24.

[6] Anonymous. 'Reviews: 69th Annual Report of the Inspectors of Lunatics (Ireland) for the year 1919'. *Journal of Mental Science* 1921; 67: 340-2; p. 340.

[7] Reynolds, *Grangegorman*; p. 219.

[8] Dawson, W.R., 'The work of the Belfast War Hospital (1917-1919)'. *Journal of Mental Science* 1925; 71: 219-24; pp. 219-20.

[9] Richardson, N.A., *Coward if I Return, A Hero if I Fall: Stories of Irishmen in World War I.* Dublin: The O'Brien Press, 2010; p. 337. See also: Lynch, S., 'Human tales bring home reality of Irish role in WWI'. *Irish Times* 2014; June 19.

[10] Boyd Barrett, E., 'Modern psycho-therapy and our asylums'. *Studies* 1924; 8: 29-43; p. 29.

[11] Reynolds, *Grangegorman*; pp. 262-3.

[12] Hinsie, L.E, Campbell, R.J., *Psychiatric Dictionary* (Fourth Edition). New York, London and Toronto: Oxford University Press, 1970; p. 785.

[13] Shorter, E., *A History of Psychiatry: From the Era of the Asylum to the Age of Prozac.* New York: John Wiley and Sons, 1997.

[14] Kelly, B.D. 'Physical sciences and psychological medicine: The legacy of Prof John Dunne'. *Irish Journal of Psychological Medicine* 2005; 22: 67-72.

[15] Dunne, J., 'The Contribution of the Physical Sciences to Psychological Medicine'. *Journal of Mental Science* 1956; 102: 209-20; Kelly, B.D., 'Physical sciences and psychological medicine: The legacy of Prof John Dunne'. *Irish Journal of Psychological Medicine* 2005; 22: 67-72.

[16] Dunne, J., 'Survey of modern physical methods of treatment for mental illness carried out in Grangegorman Mental Hospital'. *Journal of the Medical Association of Eire* 1950; 27: 4–9; p. 4.

[17] Millon, T., *Masters of the Mind: Exploring the Story of Mental Illness from Ancient Times to the New Millennium.* Hoboken, New Jersey: John Wiley and Sons, Inc., 2004.

[18] Hinsie and Campbell, *Psychiatric Dictionary*; pp. 784-5.

[19] Reynolds, *Grangegorman*; p. 264.

[20] Dunne, J., 'Survey of modern physical methods of treatment for mental illness carried out in Grangegorman Mental Hospital'. *Journal of the Medical Association of Eire* 1950; 27: 4–9.

[21] Ibid, p. 4.

[22] Shepherd, B., *A War of Nerves: Soldiers and Psychiatrists, 1914-1994.* London: Pimlico, 2002; p. 226; Jones, E., Wessely, S., *Shell Shock to PTSD: Military Psychiatry from 1900 to the Gulf War* (Maudsley Monographs

47). East Sussex, UK: Psychology Press (Taylor & Francis Group) on behalf of The Maudsley, 2005; pp. 71, 73.

[23] Stafford-Clark, D., *Psychiatry To-day*. Harmondsworth, Middlesex: Penguin Books, 1952; p. 200.

[24] Kalinowsky, L.B., 'Somatic therapy of depression'. In: Wortis, J. (ed) *Recent Advances in Biological Psychiatry Including a Havelock Ellis Centenary Symposium on Sexual Behavior* (The Proceedings of the Fourteenth Annual Convention and Scientific Program of the Society of Biological Psychiatry, Atlantic City, June 1959) (pp. 236-47). New York and London: Grune and Stratton, 1960.

[25] Sargant, W., Slater, E., *An Introduction to Physical Methods of Treatment in Psychiatry* (Fourth Edition). Edinburgh and London: E&S Livingstone, 1963.

[26] Hays, P., *New Horizons in Psychiatry*. Harmondsworth, Middlesex: Penguin Books, 1964; p. 107.

[27] Shepherd, *A War of Nerves*; p. 338.

[28] El-Hai, J., *The Lobotomist: A Maverick Medical Genius and His Tragic Quest to Rid the World of Mental Illness*. Hoboken, New Jersey: Wiley and Sons, 2005.

[29] Hinsie and Campbell, *Psychiatric Dictionary*; p. 438.

[30] Stafford-Clark, *Psychiatry To-day*; p. 201.

[31] Sargant and Slater, *An Introduction to Physical Methods of Treatment in Psychiatry*; p. 134.

[32] Shepherd, *A War of Nerves*; pp. 335-8; Jones and Wessely, *Shell Shock to PTSD*; p. 73.

[33] Reynolds, *Grangegorman*; pp. 264-5; Guéret, M., *What the Doctor Saw*. Dublin: Irish Medical Directory, 2013.

[34] Dunne, J., 'Survey of modern physical methods of treatment for mental illness carried out in Grangegorman Mental Hospital'. *Journal of the Medical Association of Eire* 1950; 27: 4–9; pp. 7-8.

[35] Reynolds, *Grangegorman*; p. 265.

[36] Dunne, J., 'Survey of modern physical methods of treatment for mental illness carried out in Grangegorman Mental Hospital'. *Journal of the Medical Association of Eire* 1950; 27: 4–9; p. 8.

[37] Stafford-Clark, *Psychiatry To-day*; pp. 201-4.

[38] Hays, *New Horizons in Psychiatry*; p. 117.

[39] El-Hai, *The Lobotomist*.

[40] Guéret, *What the Doctor Saw*.

[41] Shorter, *A History of Psychiatry*.

[42] Shorter, E., Healy, D., *Shock Therapy: A History of Electroconvulsive Treatment in Mental Illness*. New Brunswick, New Jersey and London: Rutgers University Press, 2007.

[43] McCrae, N., "A violent thunderstorm': Cardiazol treatment in British mental hospitals'. *History of Psychiatry* 2006; 17: 67-90.

[44] Meduna, L.J. von, 'Versuche über die biologische Beeinflussung des Aflaubes der Schizophrenie'. *Zeitschrift für die gesamte Neurologie und Psychiatrie* 1935; 152: 235–62.

[45] McCrae, N., "A violent thunderstorm': Cardiazol treatment in British mental hospitals'. *History of Psychiatry* 2006; 17: 67-90.

[46] Davoren, M., Breen, E.G., Kelly, B.D., 'Dr Ada English: Patriot and psychiatrist in early 20th century Ireland'. *Irish Journal of Psychological Medicine* 2011; 28: 91-6; Kelly, B.D., *Ada English: Patriot and Psychiatrist*. Sallins, Co Kildare: Irish Academic Press, 2014.

[47] Shepherd, *A War of Nerves*; pp. 76-8, 131, 309.

[48] Jones and Wessely, *Shell Shock to PTSD*; p. 73.

[49] Reynolds, *Grangegorman*; p. 264.

[50] Dunne, J., 'Survey of modern physical methods of treatment for mental illness carried out in Grangegorman Mental Hospital'. *Journal of the Medical Association of Eire* 1950; 27: 4–9; p. 4.

[51] Ibid, p. 4.

[52] Anonymous. Irish Division. *Journal of Mental Science* 1917; 63: 297-9; Reynolds, *Grangegorman*; pp. 218-9.

[53] National Institute for Clinical Excellence. *Guidance on the Use of Electroconvulsive Therapy* (Update: May 2010). London: National Institute for Clinical Excellence, 2010; p. 5.

[54] Gabbard, G.O., Kay, J., 'The fate of integrated treatment'. *American Journal of Psychiatry* 2001; 158:1956-63.

[55] Reynolds, *Grangegorman*; p. 267.

[56] Kelly, B.D., 'The Mental Treatment Act 1945 in Ireland: An historical enquiry'. *History of Psychiatry* 2008; 19: 47-67.

[57] Lyons, F.S.L., *Ireland Since the Famine*. London: Fontana, 1985.

[58] Kelly, B.D., 'Physical sciences and psychological medicine: The legacy of Prof John Dunne'. *Irish Journal of Psychological Medicine* 2005; 22: 67-72.

[59] Reynolds, *Grangegorman*; pp. 296-7.

[60] Dunne, J., 'Survey of modern physical methods of treatment for mental illness carried out in Grangegorman Mental Hospital'. *Journal of the Medical Association of Eire* 1950; 27: 4–9; Dunne, J., 'The Contribution of the Physical Sciences to Psychological Medicine'. *Journal of Mental Science* 1956; 102: 209-20; Kelly, B.D., 'Physical sciences and psychological medicine: The legacy of Prof John Dunne'. *Irish Journal of Psychological Medicine* 2005; 22: 67-72.

[61] Dunne, J., 'Out-patient psychiatric clinic – report of two years' work'. *Journal of the Irish Medical Association* 1971; 64: 7-9.

[62] Browne, I., *Music and Madness*. Cork: Atrium/Cork University Press, 2008; p. 128.

[63] Ibid, p. 131.

[64] Ibid, p. 144.

[65] Shorter, *A History of Psychiatry*.

[66] Sargant and Slater, *An Introduction to Physical Methods of Treatment in Psychiatry*; p. 23.

[67] Hinsie and Campbell, *Psychiatric Dictionary*; p. 569.

[68] Mackay, R.P., 'The neurology of motivation'. In: Wortis, J. (ed) *Recent Advances in Biological Psychiatry Including a Havelock Ellis Centenary Symposium on Sexual Behavior* (The Proceedings of the Fourteenth Annual Convention and Scientific Program of the Society of Biological Psychiatry, Atlantic City, June 1959) (pp. 2-13). New York and London: Grune and Stratton, 1960; p. 10.

[69] Hays, *New Horizons in Psychiatry*; pp. 90-1.

[70] Viney, M., 'Mental illness: An enquiry'. *Irish Times* 1968; October 23-30.

[71] *Irish Times*, 23 October 1968.

[72] Reynolds, *Grangegorman*.

[73] Department of Health. *The Psychiatric Services – Planning for the Future*. Dublin: The Stationery Office, 1984.

[74] Reynolds, *Grangegorman*; pp. 218-9.

[75] Browne, I., *Music and Madness*. Cork: Atrium/Cork University Press, 2008; pp. 148-9.

[76] Ibid, pp. 149-50.

[77] Department of Health. *Planning for the Future*.

[78] Kelly, B.D., 'Mental health policy in Ireland, 1984-2004: Theory, overview and future directions'. *Irish Journal of Psychological Medicine* 2004; 21: 61-8.

[79] Mental Health Commission. *Annual Report 2002*. Dublin: The Mental Health Commission, 2003.

[80] Swanwick, G., Lawlor, B., 'Services for dementia sufferers and their carers: Implications for future development'. In: Leahy, A.L., Wiley, M.M., (eds) *The Irish Health System in the 21st Century* (pp. 199-220). Dublin: Oak Tree Press, 1998.

[81] Inspector of Mental Hospitals. *Report of the Inspector of Mental Hospitals for the Year Ending 31st December 2003*. Dublin: Department of Health and Children, 2004.

[82] Ibid, p. 85.

[83] Ibid, p. 5.

[84] Expert Group on Mental Health Policy. *A Vision for Change: Report of the Expert Group on Mental Health Policy*. Dublin: The Stationery Office, 2006.

[85] Guruswamy, S., Kelly, B.D., 'A change of vision? Mental health policy'. *Irish Medical Journal* 2006; 99: 164-6.

[86] Expert Group on Mental Health Policy, *A Vision for Change*; p. 219.

[87] O'Brien, C., 'Goodbye Grangegorman'. *Irish Times* 2013; February 23.

# 6

# The Legacy of the Richmond War Hospital

The history of mental disorders occasioned by the First World War, and the history of shell shock in particular, are complex and important histories, indelibly linked with social, political and cultural circumstances, issues of class and gender, and the history of war itself.[1] In this context, the legacy of the Richmond War Hospital is satisfyingly multi-layered and complex to unravel. This book examines the history of the Richmond War Hospital from one particular perspective, that of medical history, and focuses especially on the War Hospital's place in the history of Ireland's remarkable asylum system and, as the title suggests, shell shock and its treatment at the War Hospital.

There are, however, other histories to be explored in relation to the War Hospital from the perspectives of sociology, military studies and cultural history, among others. There is, in particular, further work to be done in relation to public attitudes to Ireland's returning soldiers, especially those with shell shock. For the purposes of the present book, however, the legacy of the Richmond War Hospital in the context of medical history can be usefully considered in terms of three key components:

- The legacy of the Richmond War Hospital to the Irish asylum system and, especially, efforts at reform during the 1900s;

- The broader effects of the network of war hospitals throughout Great Britain and Ireland (including the Richmond War Hospital) on the identity and practice of psychiatry; and,

- The legacy of the Richmond War Hospital to Ireland's memory and commemoration of the First World War, and especially the psychological effect of the war on Irish soldiers.

Each of these legacies merits careful consideration and thought.

## The Legacy of the Richmond War Hospital to the Irish Asylum System

In the early 1900s, Ireland's asylum system comprised an expansive network of large asylums, which, in 1916, housed approximately 20,000 patients,[2] many of whom would spend lengthy periods behind asylum walls, with limited access to treatment.[3] By way of contrast, inpatient stays at the Richmond War Hospital were generally brief and treatment outcomes recorded as generally positive. By the time the War Hospital closed on 23 December 1919, 362 patients had been treated, and RMS Donelan reported that more than half 'were successfully treated and enabled to return to their homes', although he also noted that treatment was not of benefit for one-quarter of the patients admitted.[4] In addition, other soldiers were treated elsewhere in Ireland during this period, including Leopardstown Hospital (Dublin),[5] Hermitage Hospital (Lucan)[6] and Belfast War Hospital, where similarly positive results were reported.[7]

Notwithstanding the apparent therapeutic successes at the Richmond War Hospital, however, few patients returned to active army duty. In his 1925 paper in the *Journal of Mental Science*, Dawson, 'specialist in nerve diseases to the troops in Ireland', pointed out that, of the 362 patients treated at the Richmond War Hospital, 'about two-thirds were discharged to their friends or to ordinary military hospitals, two returned to duty [0.6 per cent], and only 31 were sent directly to civil asylums.'[8] This is very similar to outcomes recorded at Belfast War Hospital where, of the 1,215 admissions over 2½ years, just 18 (1.5 per cent) returned to military duty.

Statistics were similar at other war hospitals including, for example, the Red Cross Military Hospital at Maghull in England:

> It is evident that the outcome in the war neuroses is good from a medical point of view and poor from a military point of view. It is the opinion of all those consulted that, with the end of the war, most cases, even the most severe, will speedily recover, those who do not being the constitutionally neurotic and patients who have been so badly managed that very unfavourable habit-reactions have developed. This cheering fact brings little consolation, however, to those who are chiefly concerned with the wastage of fighting men.[9]

Despite the low rate of return to military duty, however, that fact remains that majorities of patients in both the Richmond and Belfast War Hospitals were discharged to families and friends within months of admission, and this marked a significant change from Ireland's general asylum system, where length of stay was commonly, although not invariably, longer.[10] This feature of the war hospitals, which was evident not just for those patients with shell shock but also those with other mental disorders, was an indicator of the potential for similar, positive change and reform throughout Ireland's broader asylum system in the future.

Another positive element of the legacy of the Richmond War Hospital relates to the manner in which its patients were treated. While the War Hospital was co-located with the Richmond District Asylum, and was subject to its administrative procedures in certain respects, it was also separate from the general asylum in important ways. In terms of treatments, one innovative aspect of the War Hospital was, as Reynolds points out, the level of 'cooperation and involvement of voluntary organisations in the care of the patients'; these groups included the Irish Automobile Club, the Irish Red Cross Society, the Royal Artillery Medical Corps and others.[11] Thus, while:

> ... singers and dramatic groups had visited the asylum in the past and had entertained the patients, the involvement of the voluntary groups with the war hospital was more regular and sustained. Later such cooperation was to be developed for the asylum at large, helping in some way to make life less claustrophobic for the patients.[12]

In this way, the Richmond War Hospital pointed to a direction for future changes in Irish asylum practice, especially with regard to enhanced therapeutic and recreational provision for patients. Even more significantly, perhaps, the Richmond War Hospital also pointed towards future innovation in relation to admission procedures and the legal status of patients in asylums. As RMS Donelan pointed out at the time, a majority of the Richmond War Hospital's patients were restored to good mental health without ever being certified insane, and this held lessons for Ireland's asylum system more generally:

> It would seem that, in dealing with many cases other than soldiers, some such system of preliminary uncertified treatment might be adopted with beneficial results to the community and save many from the blemish of having been certified insane.[13]

This was an important point. In the early 1900s, Ireland's asylums were still large, unsanitary, overcrowded and highly stigmatising places.[14] These institutions were seen, not without reason, as primarily places of detention and it was to take many more decades, and much reform work, before a voluntary admission status was firmly and clearly established, thus reducing the stigma of psychiatric hospitalisation. The need for voluntary admission status was strongly emphasized in 1927 by the *Report of the Commission on the Relief of the Sick and Destitute Poor including the Insane Poor*, which recommended the establishment of a system of auxiliary mental hospitals in old workhouses, the development of outpatient treatment programmes, and introduction of a voluntary admission status.[15] These recommendations, along with legislative developments in other countries, had a significant influence on the drafting of the Mental Treatment Act 1945.[16]

In the decades leading up to the 1945 Act, both the United Kingdom (1930) and Northern Ireland (1932) had already introduced relatively liberal mental health legislation which included, among other measures, voluntary admission status.[17] This trend towards substantial reform of mental health legislation was apparent in many other jurisdictions during this time, too: in 1936 and 1939, Switzerland, for example, passed laws that drew an increasingly clear distinction between *admissions libres* which were requested by the patient and other admissions which were requested by third parties such as parents, authorities, etc.[18] In Ireland, the clear enunciation of a voluntary admission status in the Mental Treatment Act 1945 was an important, if belated, step in the same direction – a step which would help many patients avoid 'the blemish of having been certified insane' which, as Donelan correctly pointed out, had been successfully avoided at the Richmond War Hospital, almost three decades prior to Ireland's 1945 legislation.[19]

In these ways, the Richmond War Hospital had important links with subsequent changes in the Irish asylum system more generally throughout the 1900s, chiefly as an exemplar of key reforms and promoting voluntary admission status in order to avoid the stigma of involuntary detention. Even more broadly, however, the Richmond War Hospital, as part of the larger network of war hospitals throughout Ireland and Great Britain, contributed significantly to the evolution of the practice of psychiatry in Ireland and elsewhere during this period, and this is considered next.

## The Legacy of the War Hospitals to Psychiatry

The network of war hospitals established during the First World War to treat mental symptoms among soldiers had interesting and lasting effects on the emergent discipline of psychiatry in the early twentieth century. Shell shock, in particular, forced doctors and others to realise that even 'normal' people could break down in situations of sufficient trauma and stress.[20] This idea was in stark contrast to the theory of degeneration; i.e. the idea that mental illness was largely biological and genetic in origin; worsened with each generational cycle; and was accompanied by particular physical features, such as the allegedly 'very small' head described in relation to Private FG at the Richmond War Hospital (Chapter Three).[21] As a result, the experiences of the First World War prefigured significantly the emergence of hybrid models of bio-psycho-social psychiatry later in the twentieth century.[22]

Consistent with this increased recognition of psychological factors in producing mental illness, the experience of shell shock, and the treatments that evolved to manage it, also generated new scope for the practice of psychotherapy, much of which, in retrospect, appears more aligned with later movements into cognitive therapy rather than the more analytic Freudian approaches which had been so evident up until then.[23] This was a remarkable and ground-shifting change for the discipline of psychiatry, and one which prefigured the emergence of cognitive and behavioural therapies as the dominant therapeutic paradigms later in the twentieth century.

Most interestingly, perhaps, the First World War, and the psychological symptoms its soldiers experienced, provided further evidence that there was *not* always an identifiable physical cause for psychological symptoms. This was an important realisation, both within and outside of psychiatric circles. And, in Ireland, experiences at the Richmond War Hospital made an important contribution to this debate.

At the spring 1917 meeting of the Irish Division of the MPA, the chairman, Dr Thomas Drapes (1847–1919), RMS of the Enniscorthy Asylum, County Wexford (1883–1919),[24] expressed gratitude for a detailed account of the Richmond War Hospital presented by Donelan and Forde, and went on to reflect on the folly of 'psychophysical parallelism', or, in other words, the spurious division between mental and physical symptoms, in medicine:

> He [Drapes] had not had much opportunity himself of observing cases of shell shock, as, although a few soldiers had been admitted into Enniscorthy Asylum during the past two years, some were very transient cases due to a bout of drinking: others had had previous attacks, and would probably have broken down under any stress, whether they were in the army or not. He thought that the military medical experience of the present war ought to go far towards finally disposing of the so-called theory of psychophysical parallelism, as almost every possible symptom, whether purely somatic, nervous, or mental, was found to follow shock to the brain, so that it would be quite impossible to determine where 'bodily' symptoms ended or mental began. They all were the results of similar causes, and there was no line of demarcation between them. A great many of these cases were, in their symptomatology,

very much akin to hysteria, and similar treatment to that employed in hysterical cases would be likely to prove efficacious.[25]

Drapes was a distinguished figure in Irish and British asylum-medicine, who became co-editor of the *Journal of Mental Science* in 1912 and editor-in-chief in 1915.[26] He had been elected president of the MPA in 1911/12 but had declined on health grounds. With this background, Drapes's emphasis on the continuity between physical and mental symptoms was both influential and prescient, and prefigured many of the developments in psychiatry in the twentieth century following the end of the First World War.

Finally, the First World War had various other, more subtle effects on psychiatry more generally, ranging from shaping evolving attitudes towards the psychological effects of the prisoner of war experience (Chapter Three), to assisting in the establishment of psychiatry as a respected profession within medicine. In the Irish context, however, one of the most interesting aspects of the story of the Richmond War Hospital – and, especially, how that story was been largely forgotten in the decades following the war – relates to Ireland's collective memory of the First World War itself.

## The Legacy of the Richmond War Hospital to Ireland's Memory of the First World War

The legacy and memory of the Richmond War Hospital occupy a unique position in Ireland's evolving relationship to the First World War and, in particular, historical recognition of the contribution made by the Irish to the war effort. This legacy is especially apparent in light of public discussion of Ireland's role in the war occasioned by the hundredth anniversary of its commencement in 2014.

Most vividly, public discussion in 2014 included especially detailed and moving considerations of the psychological effects of the war on Irish soldiers. These enduring effects, and the resultant need for treatment, had already been recognised, at least to a certain extent, during the war (for example, at the Richmond War Hospital) and in its immediate aftermath.[27] In 1929, for example, Liam O'Flaherty's novel, *Return of the Brute*, provided a vivid description of the psychological effects of battle, likely based, at least in part, on O'Flaherty's own traumatic experiences of the war.[28]

In 1927, the *Irish Times* reported on the death of an ex-military officer whose body was found in the River Nore, and noted that 'he suffered from shell-shock, and from time to time was much depressed'.[29] The deceased had left a note on the river bank prior to his death, and a doctor testified to the coroner that he had recommended the deceased 'about a month ago for treatment in a nerve hospital. [The deceased] had been suffering from neurasthenia since 1918, but never struck him as being a person with any tendency to commit suicide'. The jury concluded that the deceased had 'died from drowning, brought about by acute nervous depression, and they expressed sympathy' with his relatives.

In similar fashion, a century after the war commenced, Elaine Byrne wrote an especially moving article about her great-grandfather, Sylvester James Cummins, who enlisted with the 9th battalion of the Royal Dublin Fusiliers in September 1914 and was involved in three major operations including the Somme, in September 1916. After working for lengthy periods within range of enemy fire and being exposed to a gas attack at Hulluch, near Loos in France, Cummins returned from the battlefield, having 'survived the war, but not the consequences of it'.[30] For 20 years, Cummins was haunted by the noise of shelling and the smell of poison gas. In the end, his death certificate read: 'Suicide by gas poisoning, there being no evidence to show state of mind'.

Edward Byrne, father of broadcaster Gay Byrne, also served in the First World War and survived the first and second battles of Ypres, as well as the Somme, only to remain haunted by what he had experienced:

> [Gay] Byrne says his abiding memory of growing up on Rialto Street was his father waking, screaming, in the middle of the night – terror that his son believes was caused by the trauma of the war. Many who lived through the conflict never spoke about it afterwards. 'I regret we never had an adult conversation about the war,' says Byrne of his father, who died in 1952.[31]

The silence of many soldiers following the war may be attributable to a desire to forget, the cognitive effects of war trauma on memory, or a belief that the true horror of what these soldiers had seen was impossible to convey to anyone who had not been there.[32] The Richmond War Hospital aimed to deal with some of these kinds of traumas, as well as other forms of mental illness, in the immediate aftermath of soldiers' return from the war. While it is difficult to establish the precise extent to which soldiers benefitted from their treatment at the War Hospital in the long term, there can be little doubt about the good intentions of the staff, the relatively benign treatment regime,[33] and the RMS's heart-felt assertion that a majority of patients benefitted from their time there.[34]

The silence that Byrne describes following the war was, perhaps, a factor in perpetuating suffering among those who returned and grieving among the families of those who did not. That silence was significantly broken in the run up to the hundredth anniversary of the start of the war, which saw significant public recognition of the contribution of Irish soldiers.

In May 2011, Queen Elizabeth II visited Ireland and placed a wreath at the National War Memorial in Islandbridge, to remember the 40,000 Irish soldiers who died in the First World War.[35] Three years later, in 2014, the Irish President, Michael D. Higgins, visited England and, on 8 April, addressed the Houses of Parliament in Westminster, referring significantly to the First World War:

> This year the United Kingdom commemorates the First World War. In Ireland too, we remember the large number of our countrymen who entered the battlefields of Europe, never to return home. Amongst those was the Irish nationalist MP Tom Kettle who wrote that:
>
> > 'this tragedy of Europe may be and must be the prologue to the two reconciliations of which all statesmen have dreamed, the reconciliation of Protestant Ulster with Ireland, and the reconciliation of Ireland with Great Britain.'
>
> It is, I think, significant that Kettle refers to 'this tragedy of Europe'. We must always remember that this brutal and tragic war laid the hand of death on every country in Europe.
>
> Kettle died as an Irish patriot, a British soldier and a true European. He understood that to be authentically Irish we must also embrace our European identity. It is an identification we proudly claim today, an identification we share with the United Kingdom, with whom we have sat around the negotiating table in Europe for over 40 years. We recognise that it has been in that European context of mutuality and interdependence that we took the most significant steps towards each other.

... In the final days of his life, the soldier and parliamentarian, to whom I have referred, Tom Kettle dreamed of a new era of friendship between our two peoples – 'Free, we are free to be your friend' – was how he put it in one of his poems.[36]

From an historical perspective, then, growing awareness of the contribution of the Irish to the First World War has featured significantly in diplomacy between Ireland and Great Britain, especially from 2011 onwards. This has been complemented by a deepening awareness of the cost of the war to Ireland, and especially its cost in terms of human lives lost and lives marred by the lingering effects of war. The Richmond War Hospital occupies an important place in this history, testifying to an awareness of the psychological effects of the First World War and efforts made to ameliorate shell shock and other conditions in those affected.

In another way, the case histories from the Richmond War Hospital presented in this book bear witness not only to the psychological effects of the First World War, but the traumatising effects of *all* war, regardless of the era in which it occurs. Some hundred years after the First World War, accounts of the psychological effects of the Iraq war still bear strong resemblances to clinical case histories from the First World War, including nightmares, flashbacks, insomnia, depression, agitation and, in some cases, suicide.[37] One hundred years after the First World War, the term 'shell shock' has cycled out of use, replaced, in certain respects, by 'PTSD'. But regardless of what terminology is used, it remains as clear as ever that military conflict can have enduring effects on the mental health of soldiers and that specialised treatment can be needed.

In Ireland at the time of the First World War, that treatment was provided at the Richmond War Hospital and, later, Belfast War Hospital, among other locations.[38] These were complex institutions that reported high recovery rates, pointed the way for future reform of Ireland's asylum system and brought positive changes to the practice of psychiatry throughout Ireland and Great Britain.

Today, their legacies can help deepen Ireland's memory of the psychological effects of the First World War on the Irish. For all of these reasons, few could disagree with Dawson's over-all conclusions, in 1925, about the Richmond War Hospital and its Belfast counterpart:

> At all events, I think it has been shown that neither institution could easily have been dispensed with, and that both in their varying degrees have deserved well of the country, and of the brave men who sacrificed so much in defending it.[39]

## Endnotes

[1] Reid, F., *Broken Men: Shell Shock, Treatment and Recovery in Britain, 1914-30*. London and New York: Continuum International Publishing Group, 2010.

[2] Brennan, D., *Irish Insanity, 1800-2000* (Routledge Advances in Sociology). Abingdon, Oxon: Routledge, 2014; p. 124.

[3] Boyd Barrett, E., 'Modern psycho-therapy and our asylums'. *Studies* 1924; 8: 29-43.

[4] Quoted in: Reynolds, J., *Grangegorman: Psychiatric Care in Dublin since 1815*. Dublin: Institute of Public Administration in association with Eastern Health Board, 1992; p. 219. Treatment of shell shock did, however continue to generate controversy (see, for example: 'War service victims', *Irish Times*, 12 September 1922).

[5] 'Victims of the War', *Irish Times*, 19 June 1924. See also: Bourke, J., 'Shell-shock, psychiatry and the Irish soldier during the First World War'. In: Gregory, A., Pašeta, S. (eds), *Ireland and the Great War: 'A War to Unite Us All'?* (pp. 155-70). Manchester and New York: Manchester University Press, 2002.

[6] See the *Irish Times* (11 October 1918) in relation to the treatment of shell shock at the Hermitage, Lucan, which reportedly achieved 'excellent results' in such cases; see also: 'A Grand Red Cross Fete & Horse-Jumping Competition' (*Irish Times*, 9 August 1917).

[7] Dawson, W.R., 'The work of the Belfast War Hospital (1917-1919)'. *Journal of Mental Science* 1925; 71: 219-24; pp. 219-20.

[8] Ibid.

[9] Salmon, T.W., *The Care and Treatment of Mental Diseases and War Neuroses ('Shell Shock') in the British Army*. New York: War Work Committee of the National Committee for Mental Hygiene, Inc., 1917; pp. 41-2.

[10] Walsh, D., 'The ups and downs of schizophrenia in Ireland'. *Irish Journal of Psychiatry* 1992; 13: 12-6; Walsh, O., 'Gender and insanity in nineteenth-century Ireland'. *Clio Medica* 2004; 73: 69-93.

[11] Reynolds, *Grangegorman*; p. 218.

[12] Reynolds, *Grangegorman*; pp. 218-9.

[13] Quoted in: Reynolds, *Grangegorman*; p. 218.

[14] Kelly, B.D., 'One hundred years ago: The Richmond Asylum, Dublin in 1907'. *Irish Journal of Psychological Medicine* 2007; 24: 108–14; Kelly, B.D., 'Mental health law in Ireland, 1945 to 2001: Reformation and renewal'. *Medico-Legal Journal* 2008; 76: 65-72.

[15] O'Neill, A-M., *Irish Mental Health Law*. Dublin: First Law, 2005.

[16] Kelly, B.D., 'The Mental Treatment Act 1945 in Ireland: An historical enquiry'. *History of Psychiatry* 2008; 19: 47-67.

[17] O'Neill, A-M., *Irish Mental Health Law*. Dublin: First Law, 2005.

[18] Gasser, J., Heller, G., 'The confinement of the insane in Switzerland, 1900-1970: Cery (Vaud) and Bel-Air (Geneva) asylums'. In: Porter, R., Wright, D. (eds), *The Confinement of the Insane: International Perspectives, 1800-1965* (pp. 54-78). Cambridge: Cambridge University Press, 2003.

[19] Quoted in: Reynolds, *Grangegorman*; p. 218.

[20] Howorth, P., 'The treatment of shell shock: Cognitive therapy before its time'. *Psychiatric Bulletin* 2000; 24: 225-7.

[21] Shorter, E., *A History of Psychiatry: From the Era of the Asylum to the Age of Prozac*. New York: John Wiley and Sons, 1997; pp. 93-4.

[22] Gabbard, G.O., Kay, J., 'The fate of integrated treatment'. *American Journal of Psychiatry* 2001; 158:1956-63.

[23] Howorth, P., 'The treatment of shell shock: Cognitive therapy before its time'. *Psychiatric Bulletin* 2000; 24: 225-7.

[24] Walsh, D., 'Thomas Drapes, Medical Superintendent of the Enniscorthy Asylum'. *British Journal of Psychiatry* 2011; 199: 218.

[25] Anonymous. Irish Division. *Journal of Mental Science* 1917; 63: 297-9; p. 299.

[26] Walsh, D., 'Thomas Drapes, Medical Superintendent of the Enniscorthy Asylum'. *British Journal of Psychiatry* 2011; 199: 218.

[27] See, for example: 'War service victims', *Irish Times*, 12 September 1922.

[28] O'Flaherty, L., *Return of the Brute*. London: The Mandrake Press, 1929.

[29] *Irish Times*, 20 January 1927.

[30] Byrne, E., 'We let them be forgotten'. *Guardian* 2014; April 5.

[31] McGreevy, R., 'Gay Byrne: My father and the first World War'. *Irish Times* 2014; April 5.

[32] Howorth, P., 'The treatment of shell shock: Cognitive therapy before its time'. *Psychiatric Bulletin* 2000; 24: 225-7. For a discussion of 'collective amnesia' following the First World War, see: Richardson, N., *A Coward if I Return, A Hero if I Fall: Stories of Irishmen in World War I*. Dublin: The O'Brien Press, 2010; pp. 14-8.

[33] Anonymous. Irish Division. *Journal of Mental Science* 1917; 63: 297-9; Reynolds, Grangegorman; pp. 218-9.

[34] Quoted in: Reynolds, *Grangegorman*; p. 219.

[35] Gardner, D., 'A second act laden with symmetry and symbolism'. *Financial Times* 2014; April 12/13. The precise figure is not known; see: Ferriter, D., *The Transformation of Ireland, 1900-2000*. London: Profile Books, 2004; p. 132; McGreevy, R., 'Number of Irish in both wars unknown'. *Irish Times* 2014; June 9; Myers, K., 'Crunching the numbers and busting myths'. *History Ireland* 2014; 22: 40-1.

[36] Higgins, M.D., Address by Michael D. Higgins, President of Ireland to the Houses of Parliament, Westminster. Tuesday, 2014; April 8 (available at: www.president.ie/news/address-by-president-higgins-to-the-houses-of-parliament-westminster)

[37] Levy, B.S., Sidel, V.W., 'Adverse health consequences of the Iraq War'. *Lancet* 2013; 381: 949-58. See also: Powers, K., *The Yellow Birds*. London: Sceptre (Hodder & Stoughton, An Hachette UK company), 2012; Powers, K., *Letter Composed During a Lull in the Fighting*. New York: Little, Brown and Company (Hachette Book Group), 2014.

[38] Other locations included Leopardstown Hospital, Dublin ('Victims of the War', *Irish Times*, 19 June 1924) and Hermitage Hospital, Lucan; see the *Irish Times* (11 October 1918) in relation to the treatment of shell shock at the Hermitage, which reportedly achieved 'excellent results'; see also: 'A Grand Red Cross Fete & Horse-Jumping Competition' (*Irish Times*, 9 August 1917).

[39] Dawson, W.R., 'The work of the Belfast War Hospital (1917-1919)'. *Journal of Mental Science* 1925; 71: 219-24; p. 224.

# Bibliography

American Psychiatric Association. *Diagnostic and Statistical Manual of Mental Disorders* (5th edition). Washington DC: American Psychiatric Association, 2013.

Anonymous. 'Obituary: Joseph Lalor, MD'. *Journal of Mental Science* 1886; 32: 462-3.

Anonymous. Irish Division. *Journal of Mental Science* 1917; 63: 297-9.

Anonymous. 'Reviews: 69th Annual Report of the Inspectors of Lunatics (Ireland) for the year 1919'. *Journal of Mental Science* 1921; 67: 340-2.

Anonymous. 'Review of: The Sixth Annual Report of the Board of Control for the year 1919; history of the asylum war hospitals in England and Wales: Report to the Secretary of State for the Home Department by Sir Marriott Cooke, K.B.E., M.B., and C. Hubert Bond, C.B.E., M.D., D.Sc., F.R.C.P., Commissioners of the Board of Control'. *Journal of Mental Science* 1921; 67: 484-92.

Atenstaedt, R.L., 'Trench fever: the British medical response in the Great War'. *Journal of the Royal Society of Medicine* 2006; 99: 564–8.

Barker, P., *The Regeneration Trilogy* (Reissue). London: Viking/Penguin Group, 2014.

Barry, S., *A Long Long Way*. London, Faber and Faber Limited, 2005.

Bartlett, P., *The Poor Law of Lunacy*. London and Washington: Leicester University Press, 1999.

Barton White, E., 'Abstract of a report on the mental division of the Welsh Metropolitan War Hospital, Whitchurch, Cardiff, September, 1917–September, 1919'. *Journal of Mental Science* 1920; 66: 438-49.

Bewley, T. *Madness to Mental Illness: A History of the Royal College of Psychiatrists*. London: Royal College of Psychiatrists, 2008.

Bisson, J., Andrew, M., 'Psychological treatment of post-traumatic stress disorder (PTSD): *Cochrane Database of Systematic Reviews* 2007; 18: CD003388.

Bourke, J., 'Shell-shock, psychiatry and the Irish soldier during the First World War'. In: Gregory, A., Pašeta, S. (eds), *Ireland and the Great War: 'A War to Unite Us All'?* (pp. 155-70). Manchester and New York: Manchester University Press, 2002.

Boyd Barrett, E., 'Modern psycho-therapy and our asylums'. *Studies* 1924; 8: 29-43.

Braslow, J.T., 'Punishment or therapy. Patients, doctors, and somatic remedies in the early twentieth century'. *Psychiatric Clinics of North America* 1994; 17: 493-513.

Breckenridge, A., 'William Withering's legacy – for the good of the patient'. *Clinical Medicine* 2006; 6: 393-7.

Brennan, D., *Irish Insanity, 1800-2000* (Routledge Advances in Sociology). Abingdon, Oxon: Routledge, 2014.

Brown, E.M., 'Why Wagner-Jauregg won the Nobel Prize for discovering malaria therapy for general paralysis of the insane'. *History of Psychiatry* 2000; 11: 371-82.

Browne, I., *Music and Madness*. Cork: Atrium/Cork University Press, 2008.

Brune, K., 'The early history of non-opioid analgesics'. *Acute Pain* 1997; 1: 33-40.

Byrne, E., 'We let them be forgotten'. *Guardian* 2014; April 5.

Carlson, E.T., Dain, N., 'The psychotherapy that was moral treatment'. *American Journal of Psychiatry* 1960; 117: 519-24.

*Census of Ireland for the Year 1851 (Part III)*. Dublin: Thom and Sons, for Her Majesty's Stationery Office, 1854.

Cherry, S., Munting, R., '"Exercise is the thing"? Sport and the Asylum c1850-1950'. *International Journey of the History of Sport* 2005; 22: 42-58.

Clare, A.W., 'St. Patrick's Hospital'. *American Journal of Psychiatry* 1998; 155: 1599.

Clarke, C.R.A., 'Neurological diseases and diseases of voluntary muscle'. In: Kumar, P., Clark, M. (eds), *Clinical Medicine* (pp. 871-955). London: Ballière Tindall, 1994.

Collins, A., *St Vincent's Hospital, Fairview: An Illustrated history, 1857-2007*. Dublin: Albertine Kennedy Publishing with Duke Kennedy Sweetman, 2007.

Collins, A., 'Eleonora Fleury captured'. *British Journal of Psychiatry* 2013; 203: 5.

Collins, A., 'The Richmond District Asylum and the 1916 Easter Rising'. *Irish Journal of Psychological Medicine* 2013; 30: 279-83.

Cooney, T., O'Neill, O., *Psychiatric Detention: Civil Commitment in Ireland* (Kritik 1). Wicklow: Baikonur, 1996.

Cox, J.M., *Practical Observations on Insanity*. London: Baldwin and Murray, 1804.

Cox, J.M., *Practical Observations on Insanity* (Second Edition). London: Baldwin and Murray, 1806.

Davoren, M., Breen, E.G., Kelly, B.D., 'Dr Adeline English: Revolutionizing politics and psychiatry in Ireland'. *Irish Psychiatrist* 2009; 10: 260-2.

Davoren, M., Breen, E.G., Kelly, B.D., 'Dr Ada English: Patriot and psychiatrist in early 20th century Ireland. *Irish Journal of Psychological Medicine* 2011; 28: 91-6.

Dawe, G. (ed)., *Earth Voices Whispering: An Anthology of Irish War Poetry, 1914–1945*. Belfast: Blackstaff Press, 2008.

Dawson, W.R., 'The work of the Belfast War Hospital (1917-1919)'. *Journal of Mental Science* 1925; 71: 219-24.

Department of Health. *The Psychiatric Services – Planning For The Future*. Dublin: The Stationery Office, 1984.

Donelan, J. O'C. Report to the Governors of the Richmond District Asylum, 1916, 11 May.

Douglas, G., Goodbody, R., Mauger, A., Davey, J., *Bloomfield: A History, 1812-2012*. Dublin: Ashfield Press, 2012.

Dungan, M., *They Shall Grow Not Old: Irish Soldiers and the Great War*. Dublin: Four Courts Press Limited, 1997.

Dunne, J., 'Survey of modern physical methods of treatment for mental illness carried out in Grangegorman Mental Hospital'. *Journal of the Medical Association of Eire* 1950; 27: 4–9.

Dunne, J., 'The Contribution of the Physical Sciences to Psychological Medicine'. *Journal of Mental Science* 1956; 102: 209-20

Dunne, J., 'Out-patient psychiatric clinic – report of two years' work'. *Journal of the Irish Medical Association* 1971; 64: 7-9.

Eager, R., 'A record of admissions to the mental section of the Lord Derby War Hospital, Warrington, from June 17th, 1916 to June 16th, 1917'. *Journal of Mental Science* 1918; 64: 272-96.

El-Hai, J., *The Lobotomist: A Maverick Medical Genius and His Tragic Quest to Rid the World of Mental Illness.* Hoboken, New Jersey: Wiley and Sons, 2005.

Elliot Smith, G., Pear, T.H., *Shell Shock and its Lessons.* London: Longmans, Green & Co., 1917.

Erichsen, J.E., *On Railway and Other Injuries of the Nervous System.* Philadelphia: Henry C. Lea, 1867.

Esquirol, J-É., *Des Passions.* Paris: Didot Jeune, 1805.

Expert Group on Mental Health Policy. *A Vision for Change: Report of the Expert Group on Mental Health Policy.* Dublin: The Stationery Office, 2006.

Farmar, T., *Patients, Potions and Physicians: A Social History of Medicine in Ireland.* Dublin: A & A Farmar in association with the Royal College of Physicians of Ireland, 2004.

Ferriter, D., *The Transformation of Ireland, 1900-2000.* London: Profile Books, 2004.

Finnane, P., *Insanity and the Insane in Post-Famine Ireland.* London: Croom Helm, 1981.

Fleetwood, J.F., *The History of Medicine in Ireland* (Second Edition). Dublin: Skellig Press, 1983.

Gabbard, G.O., Kay, J., 'The fate of integrated treatment'. *American Journal of Psychiatry* 2001; 158:1956-63.

Gardner, D., 'A second act laden with symmetry and symbolism'. *Financial Times* 2014; April 12/13.

Gasser, J., Heller, G., 'The confinement of the insane in Switzerland, 1900-1970: Cery (Vaud) and Bel-Air (Geneva) asylums'. In: Porter, R., Wright, D. (eds), *The Confinement of the Insane: International Perspectives, 1800-1965* (pp. 54-78). Cambridge: Cambridge University Press, 2003.

Gibbons, P., Mulryan, N., O'Connor, A., 'Guilty but insane: The insanity defence in Ireland, 1850–1995'. *British Journal of Psychiatry* 1997; 170: 467-72.

Greaves, C.D., *Liam Mellows and the Irish Revolution*. Belfast: An Ghlór Gafa, 2004.

Guéret, M., *What the Doctor Saw*. Dublin: Irish Medical Directory, 2013.

Guruswamy, S., Kelly, B.D., 'A change of vision? Mental health policy'. *Irish Medical Journal* 2006; 99: 164-6.

Guthrie, D., *A History of Medicine*. London: Thomas Nelson and Sons Limited, 1945.

Hallaran, W.S., *An Enquiry into the Causes Producing the Extraordinary Addition to the Number of Insane together with Extended Observations on the Cure of Insanity with Hints as to the Better Management of Public Asylums for Insane Persons*. Cork: Edwards and Savage, 1810.

Hallaran, W.S., *Practical Observations on the Causes and Cures of Insanity* (Second Edition). Cork: Edwards and Savage, 1818.

Hays, P., *New Horizons in Psychiatry*. Harmondsworth, Middlesex: Penguin Books, 1964.

Henderson, D.K., 'War psychoses: An analysis of 202 cases of mental disorder occurring in home troops'. *Journal of Mental Science* 1918; 64: 165-89.

Henry, H.M., *Our Lady's Hospital, Cork: History of the Mental Hospital in Cork Spanning 200 years*. Cork: Haven Books, 1989.

Higgins, M.D., Address by Michael D. Higgins, President of Ireland to the Houses of Parliament, Westminster.Tuesday, 2014; April 8 (available at: www.president.ie/news/address-by-president-higgins-to-the-houses-of-parliament-westminster).

Hinsie, L.E., Campbell, R.J., *Psychiatric Dictionary* (Fourth Edition). New York, London and Toronto: Oxford University Press, 1970.

Hotchkis, R.D., 'Renfrew District Asylum as a war hospital for mental invalids: Some contrasts in administration with an analysis of cases admitted during the first year'. *Journal of Mental Science* 1917; 63: 238-49.

Howorth, P., 'The treatment of shell shock: Cognitive therapy before its time'. *Psychiatric Bulletin* 2000; 24: 225-7.

Inspector of Lunatic Asylums. *Report of the District, Local and Private Lunatic Asylums in Ireland 1846.* Dublin: Alexander Thom, for Her Majesty's Stationery Office, 1847.

Inspector of Lunatics (Ireland). *The Forty-Second Report (With Appendices) of the Inspector of Lunatics (Ireland).* Dublin: Thom and Co./ Her Majesty's Stationery Office, 1893.

Inspectors of Lunatics (Ireland). *The Sixty-Fifth Annual Report (With Appendices) of the Inspectors of Lunatics (Ireland), Being for the Year Ending 31$^{st}$ December 1915.* Dublin: His Majesty's Stationery Office, 1917.

Inspectors of Lunatics (Ireland). *The Sixty-Sixth Annual Report (With Appendices) of the Inspectors of Lunatics (Ireland), Being for the Year Ending 31$^{st}$ December 1916.* Dublin: His Majesty's Stationery Office, 1918.

Inspectors of Lunatics (Ireland). *The Sixty-Seventh Annual Report (With Appendices) of the Inspectors of Lunatics (Ireland), Being for the Year Ending 31$^{st}$ December 1917.* Dublin: His Majesty's Stationery Office, 1919.

Inspector of Mental Hospitals. *Report of the Inspector of Mental Hospitals for the Year Ending 31$^{st}$ December 2003.* Dublin: Department of Health and Children, 2004.

Johnson, W., Rows, R.G., 'Neurasthenia and war neuroses'. In: MacPherson, W.G., Herringham, W.P., Elliott, T.R., Balfour, A. (eds), *History of the Great War Based on Official Documents, Volume II: Medical Services, Diseases of War* (pp. 1-67). London: HMSO, 1923.

Jones, E., 'Historical approaches to post-combat disorders'. *Philosophical Transactions of the Royal Society* B 2006; 361: 533-42.

Jones, E., Fear, N.T., Wessely, S., 'Shell shock and mild traumatic brain injury: A historical review'. *American Journal of Psychiatry* 2007; 164: 1641-5.

Jones, E., Hodgins, Vermaas R., McCartney, H., Everitt, B., Beech, C., Poynter, D., Palmer, I., Hyams, K., Wessely, S., 'Post-combat syndromes from the Boer War to the Gulf: A cluster analysis of their nature and attribution'. *British Medical Journal* 2002; 324: 321–4.

Jones, E., Wessely, S., *Shell Shock to PTSD: Military Psychiatry from 1900 to the Gulf War* (Maudsley Monographs 47). East Sussex, UK: Psychology Press (Taylor & Francis Group) on behalf of The Maudsley, 2005.

Jones, E., Wessely, S., 'British prisoners-of-war: From resilience to psychological vulnerability: Reality or perception'. *Twentieth Century British History* 2010; 21: 163-83.

Jones, G., 'The Campaign Against Tuberculosis in Ireland, 1899-1914'. In: Malcolm, E., Jones, G. (eds) *Medicine, Disease and the State in Ireland, 1650-1940* (pp. 158-76). Cork: Cork University Press, 1999.

Kalinowsky, L.B., 'Somatic therapy of depression'. In: Wortis, J. (ed) *Recent Advances in Biological Psychiatry Including a Havelock Ellis Centenary Symposium on Sexual Behavior* (The Proceedings of the Fourteenth Annual Convention and Scientific Program of the Society of Biological Psychiatry, Atlantic City, June 1959) (pp. 236-47). New York and London: Grune and Stratton, 1960

Kelly, B.D., 'Mental health policy in Ireland, 1984-2004: Theory, overview and future directions'. *Irish Journal of Psychological Medicine* 2004; 21: 61-8.

Kelly, B.D., 'Physical sciences and psychological medicine: The legacy of Prof John Dunne'. *Irish Journal of Psychological Medicine* 2005; 22: 67-72.

Kelly, B.D., 'One hundred years ago: The Richmond Asylum, Dublin in 1907'. *Irish Journal of Psychological Medicine* 2007; 24: 108–14.

Kelly, B.D., 'The Mental Treatment Act 1945 in Ireland: an historical enquiry'. *History of Psychiatry* 2008; 19: 47-67.

Kelly, B.D., 'Mental Health Law in Ireland, 1821-1902: Building the Asylums'. *Medico-Legal Journal* 2008; 76: 19-25.

Kelly, B.D., 'Mental Health Law in Ireland, 1821-1902: Dealing with the "increase of insanity in Ireland."' *Medico-Legal Journal* 2008; 76: 26-33.

Kelly, B.D., 'Mental health law in Ireland, 1945 to 2001: reformation and renewal'. *Medico-Legal Journal* 2008; 76: 65-72.

Kelly, B.D., 'Dr William Saunders Hallaran and psychiatric practice in nineteenth-century Ireland'. *Irish Journal of Medical Science* 2008; 177: 79-84.

Kelly, B.D., 'Criminal insanity in 19th-century Ireland, Europe and the United States: Cases, contexts and controversies'. *International Journal of Law and Psychiatry* 2009; 32: 362-8.

Kelly, B.D., 'Tuberculosis in the nineteenth-century asylum: Clinical cases from the Central Criminal Lunatic Asylum, Dundrum, Dublin'. In: Prior, P.M. (ed), *Asylums, Mental Health Care and the Irish, 1800-2010* (pp. 205-20). Dublin and Portland, OR: Irish Academic Press, 2011.

Kelly, B.D., *Ada English: Patriot and Psychiatrist*. Sallins, Co Kildare: Irish Academic Press, 2014.

Kelly, B.D., 'Dr Ada English (1875–1944): Doctor, patriot, politician'. *British Journal of Psychiatry* 2014; 204: 5.

Kelly, B.D., 'Integrating psychological treatment approaches'. *Science* 2014; 344; 254-5.

Kelly, B., Davoren, M., 'Dr Ada English'. In: Mulvihill, M. (ed), *Lab Coats and Lace: The Lives and Legacies of Inspiring Irish Women Scientists and Pioneers* (p. 97). Dublin: Women in Technology and Science, 2009.

Lalor, J., 'On the use of education and training in the treatment of the insane in public lunatic asylums'. *Journal of the Statistical and Social Inquiry of Ireland* 1878; 7: 361–73.

Ledwidge, F., *Francis Ledwidge: Complete Poems* (edited by Alice Curtayne). London: Martin Brian & O'Keefe, 1974.

Leonard, E.C. Jr., 'Did some 18th and 19th century treatments for mental disorders act on the brain?' *Medical Hypotheses* 2004; 62: 219-21.

Lerner, P., 'From traumatic neurosis to male hysteria: The decline and fall of Hermann Oppenheim, 1889-1919'. In: Micale, M., Lerner, P. (eds), *Traumatic Pasts: History, Psychiatry and Trauma in the Modern Age, 1870–1930* (pp. 140-71). Cambridge: Cambridge University 2001.

Levy, B.S., Sidel, V.W., 'Adverse health consequences of the Iraq War'. *Lancet* 2013; 381: 949-58.

Lynch, S., 'Human tales bring home reality of Irish role in WWI'. *Irish Times* 2014; June 19.

Lyons, F.S.L., *Ireland Since the Famine*. London: Fontana, 1985.

Mackay, R.P., 'The neurology of motivation'. In: Wortis, J. (ed), *Recent Advances in Biological Psychiatry Including a Havelock Ellis Centenary*

*Symposium on Sexual Behavior* (The Proceedings of the Fourteenth Annual Convention and Scientific Program of the Society of Biological Psychiatry, Atlantic City, June 1959) (pp. 2-13). New York and London: Grune and Stratton, 1960

Malcolm, E., *Swift's Hospital: A History of St Patrick's Hospital*, Dublin, 1746-1989. Dublin: Gill and Macmillan, 1989.

McAuley, F., *Insanity, Psychiatry and Criminal Responsibility*. Dublin: Round Hall Press, 1993.

McCandless, P., 'Curative asylum, custodial hospital: The South Carolina Lunatic Asylum and State Hospital, 1828–1920'. In: Porter, R., Wright, D. (eds), *The Confinement of the Insane: International Perspectives, 1800–1965* (pp. 173–92). Cambridge: Cambridge University Press, 2003.

McCarthy, A., *A Doctor's War*. Cork: The Collins Press, 2005.

McCarthy, C., *Cumann na mBan and the Irish Revolution*. Dublin: The Collins Press, 2007.

McCrae, N., '"A violent thunderstorm": Cardiazol treatment in British mental hospitals'. *History of Psychiatry* 2006; 17: 67-90.

McGreevy, R., 'Gay Byrne: My father and the first World War'. *Irish Times* 2014; April 5.

McGreevy, R., 'Number of Irish in both wars unknown'. *Irish Times* 2014; June 9.

Meduna, L.J. von., 'Versuche über die biologische Beeinflussung des Aflaubes der Schizophrenie'. *Zeitschrift für die gesamte Neurologie und Psychiatrie* 1935; 152: 235–62.

Mental Health Commission. *Annual Report 2002*. Dublin: The Mental Health Commission, 2003.

Merrit, H.H., Adams, R., Solomon, H.C., *Neurosyphilis*. Oxford: Oxford University Press, 1946.

Merskey, H., *The Analysis of Hysteria*. London: Gaskell, 1979.

Millon, T., *Masters of the Mind: Exploring the Story of Mental Illness from Ancient Times to the New Millennium*. Hoboken, New Jersey: John Wiley and Sons, Inc., 2004.

Mitchell, T.J., Smith, G.M., *Medical Services, Casualties, and Medical Statistics of the Great War*. London: His Majesty's Stationery Office, 1931.

Mott, F.W., 'Special discussion on shell shock without visible signs of injury'. *Proceedings of the Royal Society of Medicine* 1916; 9: i–xxiv.

Mott, F.W., 'The microscopic examination of the brains of two men dead of commotion cerebri (shell shock) without visible external injury'. *British Medical Journal* 1917; 2: 612–5.

Mulholland, M., *To Comfort Always: A History of Holywell Hospital, 1898-1998*. Ballymena: Homefirst Community Trust, 1998.

Murray, L.M., 'The common factor in disordered action of the heart'. *British Medical Journal* 1918; 2(3024): 650-2.

Myers, C.S., 'A contribution to the study of shell shock'. *Lancet* 1915; 185: 316-20.

Myers, C.S., 'Contributions to the study of shell shock: Being an account of certain disorders of cutaneous sensibility'. *Lancet* 1916; 187: 608-13.

Myers, K., 'Crunching the numbers and busting myths'. *History Ireland* 2014; 22: 40-1.

National Institute for Clinical Excellence. *Guidance on the Use of Electroconvulsive Therapy* (Update: May 2010). London: National Institute for Clinical Excellence, 2010.

Norman, J.C., *Richmond Asylum Joint Committee Minutes*. Dublin: Richmond Asylum, 1907.

O'Brien, C., 'Goodbye Grangegorman'. *Irish Times* 2013; February 23.

O'Flaherty, L., *Return of the Brute*. London: The Mandrake Press, 1929.

O'Neill, A-M., *Irish Mental Health Law*. Dublin: First Law, 2005.

Page, W.F., *The Health of Former Prisoners of War: Results from the Medical Examination Survey of Former POWs of World War II and the Korean Conflict*. Washington DC: National Academy Press, 1992.

Porter, R., 'The patient's view. Doing medical history from below'. *Theory and Society* 1985; 14: 175-98.

Porter, R., *Madmen: A Social History of Madhouses, Mad-Doctors and Lunatics*. Gloucestershire, United Kingdom: Tempus, 2004.

Powers, K., *The Yellow Birds*. London: Sceptre (Hodder & Stoughton, An Hachette UK company), 2012.

Powers, K., *Letter Composed During a Lull in the Fighting*. New York: Little, Brown and Company (Hachette Book Group), 2014.

Prior, P., 'Dangerous lunacy: The misuse of mental health law in nineteenth-century Ireland'. *Journal of Forensic Psychiatry and Psychology* 2003; 14: 525-41.

Prior, P., 'Prisoner or lunatic? The official debate on the criminal lunatic in nineteenth-century Ireland'. *History of Psychiatry* 2004; 15: 177–92.

Psychiatrist. 'Insanity in Ireland'. *The Bell* 1944; 7: 303-10.

Reid, F., *Broken Men: Shell Shock, Treatment and Recovery in Britain, 1914-30*. London and New York: Continuum International Publishing Group, 2010.

Reuber, M., 'The architecture of psychological management: The Irish asylums (1801-1922)'. *Psychological Medicine* 1996; 26: 1179–89.

Reuber, M., 'Moral management and the "unseen eye": Public lunatic asylums in Ireland, 1800–1845'. In: Malcolm, E., Jones, G. (eds), *Medicine, Disease and the State in Ireland, 1650-1940* (pp. 208–33). Cork: Cork University Press, 1999.

Reynolds, J., *Grangegorman: Psychiatric Care in Dublin since 1815*. Dublin: Institute of Public Administration in association with Eastern Health Board, 1992.

Richardson, N., *A Coward if I Return, A Hero if I Fall: Stories of Irishmen in World War I*. Dublin: The O'Brien Press, 2010.

Risse, G.B., Warner, J.H., 'Reconstructing clinical activities: Patient records in medical history'. *Social History of Medicine* 1992; 5: 183-205.

Rivers, W.H.R., 'An address on the repression of war experience'. *Lancet* 1918; i: 173-7.

Rivers, W.H.R., *Instinct and the Unconscious: A Contribution to a Biological Theory of the Psycho-Neuroses*. Cambridge: Cambridge University Press, 1920.

Robins, J., *Fools and Mad: A History of the Insane in Ireland*. Dublin: Institute of Public Administration, 1986.

Salmon, T.W., 'The care and treatment of mental diseases and war neuroses ("shell shock") in the British army'. *Mental Hygiene* 1917; 1: 509–47.

Salmon, T.W., *The Care and Treatment of Mental Diseases and War Neuroses ("Shell Shock") in the British Army*. New York: War Work Committee of the National Committee for Mental Hygiene, Inc., 1917.

Sargant, W., Slater, E., *An Introduction to Physical Methods of Treatment in Psychiatry* (Fourth Edition). Edinburgh and London: E&S Livingstone, 1963.

Shepherd, B., *A War of Nerves: Soldiers and Psychiatrists, 1914-1994*. London: Pimlico, 2002.

Shorter, E., *A History of Psychiatry: From the Era of the Asylum to the Age of Prozac*. New York: John Wiley and Sons, 1997.

Shorter, E., Healy, D., *Shock Therapy: A History of Electroconvulsive Treatment in Mental Illness*. New Brunswick, New Jersey and London: Rutgers University Press, 2007.

Smith, L., *'Cure, Comfort and Safe Custody': Public Lunatic Asylums in Early Nineteenth-Century England*. London and New York: Leicester University Press, 1999.

Smith, L., '"Your very thankful inmate": Discovering the patients of an early county lunatic asylum'. *Social History of Medicine* 2008; 21: 237-52.

Stafford-Clark, D., *Psychiatry To-day*. Harmondsworth, Middlesex: Penguin Books, 1952.

Stewart, A., 'Wilfred Owen: Hospital poet'. *British Journal of Psychiatry* 2013; 203: 195.

Stone, M.H., *Healing the Mind: A History of Psychiatry from Antiquity to the Present*. London: Pimlico, 1998.

Swanwick, G., Lawlor, B., 'Services for dementia sufferers and their carers: Implications for future development'. In: Leahy, A.L., Wiley, M.M. (eds), *The Irish Health System In The 21st Century* (pp. 199-220). Dublin: Oak Tree Press, 1998.

Thomson, D.G., 'A descriptive record of the conversion of a county asylum into a war hospital for sick and wounded soldiers in 1915'. *Journal of Mental Science* 1916; 62: 109-35.

Torrey, E., Miller, J., *The Invisible Plague: The Rise of Mental Illness from 1750 to the Present*. Piscataway, New Jersey: Rutgers University Press, 2001.

Tuke, D.H., 'On the Richmond Asylum schools'. *Journal of Mental Science* 1875; 21: 467-74.

Tuomy, M., *Treatise on the Principal Diseases of Dublin*. Dublin: William Folds, 1810.

United Nations. *Principles for the Protection of Persons with Mental Illness and the Improvement of Mental Health Care*. New York: United Nations, Secretariat Centre for Human Rights, 1991.

Vincent, W., 'Use of asylums as military hospitals'. *Journal of Mental Science* 1916; 62: 174-8.

Viney, M., 'Mental illness: An enquiry'. *Irish Times* 1968; October 23-30.

Wade, N.J., 'The original spin doctors – the meeting of perception and insanity'. *Perception* 2005; 34: 253–60.

Wade, N.J., Norrsell, U., Presly, A., 'Cox's chair "a moral and a medical mean in the treatment of maniacs"'. *History of Psychiatry* 2005; 16: 73–88.

Walker, D., 'Modern nerves, nervous moderns: Notes on male neurasthenia'. In: Goldberg, S.L., Smith, F.B., *Australian Cultural History* (pp. 123-37). Cambridge: Cambridge University Press, 1988.

Walsh, D., 'The ups and downs of schizophrenia in Ireland'. *Irish Journal of Psychiatry* 1992; 13: 12-6.

Walsh, D., 'Thomas Drapes, Medical Superintendent of the Enniscorthy Asylum'. *British Journal of Psychiatry* 2011; 199: 218.

Walsh, D., Daly, A., *Mental Illness in Ireland 1750–2002: Reflections on the Rise and Fall of Institutional Care*. Dublin: Health Research Board, 2004.

Walsh, O., 'Gender and insanity in nineteenth-century Ireland'. *Clio Medica* 2004; 73: 69-93.

War Office Committee of Enquiry into 'Shell-Shock'. *Report of the War Office Committee of Enquiry into 'Shell-Shock'*. London: HMSO, 1922.

Waugh, M.A., 'Alfred Fournier, 1832-1914: His influence on venereology'. *British Journal of Venereal Disease* 1974; 50: 232-6.

Weber, M.M., Emrich, H.M., 'Current and historical concepts of opiate treatment in psychiatric disorders'. *International Journal of Clinical Psychopharmacology* 1988; 3: 255-66.

Williamson, A.P., 'Psychiatry, moral management and the origins of social policy for mentally ill people in Ireland'. *Irish Journal of Medical Science* 1992; 161: 556-8.

World Health Organisation. *The ICD-10 Classification of Mental and Behavioural Disorders: Clinical Descriptions and Diagnostic Guidelines.* Geneva: World Health Organisation, 1992.

Wright, D., Moran, J.E., Gouglas, S., 'The confinement of the insane in Victorian Canada: The Hamilton and Toronto asylums, c. 1861–1891'. In: Porter, R., Wright, D. (eds), *The Confinement of the Insane: International Perspectives, 1800–1965* (pp. 100–28). Cambridge: Cambridge University Press, 2003.

# Acknowledgements

I am very grateful to Professor Sir Simon Wessely (President, Royal College of Psychiatrists) for writing the foreword to this book, and to Professor Ivor Browne for reading the manuscript and writing the preface.

I greatly appreciate the support and guidance of Mr David Givens of The Liffey Press.

The programme of research upon which this book is based was approved by the Ethics Committee of the Health Service Executive, Dublin North City, Ireland. I am very grateful for the assistance and support of Dr Roy Browne, Dr Margo Wrigley, Mr Sean Tone and Mr Gerry Devine (Health Service Executive, Dublin); Mr Brian Donnelly (National Archives of Ireland); Professor Patricia Casey, Dr John Sheehan, Dr Eugene Breen, Dr Aidan Collins and Dr Peter Reid (University College Dublin); Professor Ivor Browne and Dr John Bruzzi.

Particular thanks to Dr Larkin Feeney who, once again, read and advised on an earlier version of this manuscript.

I am very grateful to Professor Sharlene Walbaum, her family, colleagues and students at Quinnipiac University, Connecticut. Shar's wisdom, enthusiasm and hospitality have added greatly to my historical work.

I am also very grateful to Mr Alan Counihan for inviting me to become involved in the Personal Effects project (St. Brendan's Hospital, 2014).

I owe a long-standing debt of gratitude to my teachers at Scoil Chaitríona, Renmore, Galway; St Joseph's Patrician College, Nun's Island, Galway (especially my history teacher, Mr Ciaran Doyle); and the School of Medicine at NUI Galway.

Finally, and above all else, I deeply appreciate the support of my wife (Regina), children (Eoin and Isabel), parents (Mary and Desmond), sisters (Sinéad and Niamh) and niece (Aoife).

Some of the material presented in this book is 'in press' with the journal *History of Psychiatry*, published by SAGE Publications Ltd.

## Permissions

I am very grateful to the following for permission to reproduce published material:

- Material from the *Guardian* newspaper is reproduced by kind permission of the Guardian News & Media Ltd.

- Material from the *Irish Journal of Psychological Medicine* is reproduced by kind permission of Cambridge University Press, the College of Psychiatrists of Ireland and Dr Aidan Collins (St Vincent's Hospital, Fairview, Dublin)

- Material from the *Irish Times* is reproduced by kind permission of the *Irish Times*.

- Material from the *Journal of the Statistical and Social Inquiry of Ireland* is reproduced by kind permission of the *Journal of the Statistical and Social Inquiry of Ireland*.

- Material from the *Journal of Mental Science* is reproduced by kind permission of the Royal College of Psychiatrists.

- Material from *The ICD-10 Classification of Mental and Behavioural Disorders: Clinical Descriptions and Diagnostic Guidelines* is reproduced by kind permission of the World Health Organisation (Geneva).

- Material from the 'Reports and Analyses and Descriptions of New Inventions in Medicine, Surgery, Dietetics and the Allied Sciences' is reproduced from *British Medical Journal* with permission from BMJ Publishing Group Ltd.

- Material from *Studies* is reproduced by kind permission of the editor of *Studies*.

- Material from the address by Michael D. Higgins, President of Ireland to the Houses of Parliament, Westminster. Tuesday, 2014; April 8 is reproduced by kind permission of the Office of the President of Ireland.

- Material from *A Doctor's War* by Dr Aidan McCarthy is reproduced by kind permission of Dr McCarthy's family.

- Material from *Music and Madness* by Ivor Browne is reproduced by kind permission of Cork University Press.

- Material from *Swift's Hospital: A History of St Patrick's Hospital, Dublin, 1746-1989* by Elizabeth Malcolm is reproduced by kind permission of Gill and Macmillan.

- Material from *Grangegorman: Psychiatric Care in Dublin since 1815* by J. Reynolds is reproduced by kind permission of the Institute of Public Administration.

I am very grateful to the editors, publishers, authors and copyright holders of these publications for permitting re-use of material in this book. All reasonable efforts have been made to contact the copyright holders for all texts quoted in this book. If any have been omitted, please contact the publisher.

# Index